Leading Congregational Change Workbook

Leading Congregational Change Workbook

James H. Furr
Mike Bonem
Jim Herrington

Jossey-Bass Publishers • San Francisco

Jossey-Bass books and products are available through most bookstores. To contact Jossey-Bass directly, call (888) 378-2537, fax to (800) 605-2665, or visit our website at www.josseybass.com.

Substantial discounts on bulk quantities of Jossey-Bass books are available to corporations, professional associations, and other organizations. For details and discount information, contact the special sales department at Jossey-Bass.

ISBN   978-0-7879-4885-6

Contents

For our parents

Jack and June Furr
Joe and Diane Bonem
Jim and Helen Herrington

from whom we first learned
to love the church
with all our
hearts and minds and souls.

About This Workbook

If you keep doing what you've been doing, you'll keep getting what you've been getting. We use this expression frequently in consulting and training related to congregational change because we believe that the call for transformation is clear and emphatic. The state of Christianity in America, however, provides powerful and distressing evidence that we "keep doing what we've been doing."

Many pastors and other church leaders recognize the patterns of stagnation at the national and local levels. Leading church observers have described the struggles and characteristics of today's modern church in detail. And thousands of pastors and key leaders attend conferences every year in search of the latest quick-fix answers. The real issue, though, is not whether change is needed or even whether good models of faithful and effective churches exist at the dawn of the new millennium. Most church leaders are aware of healthy traits that they want to increase in their congregations.

Their question is how to transform their current congregation—with all of its traditions, attitudes, programs, and patterns. How can they discern God's vision and make progress toward its implementation? What are the pitfalls and risks to be avoided? What skills are essential to ongoing transformation? These are the issues that separate the many churches struggling with transformation from the few that have done so successfully.

This workbook is a complement to *Leading Congregational Change: A Practical Guide for the Transformational Journey*. Significant transformation is a challenging process. The book examines this process in depth and answers many of the questions that congregations ask as they engage in transformation. The workbook provides leaders with frameworks for assessing what changes are needed. It suggests specific tools and methods for initiating and guiding change. It is designed as a sourcebook for ongoing process guidance and skill development, and as a place for leaders to note their observations during a long transformational journey. As leaders use this workbook, congregations will develop customized strategies for their unique context and calling.

The sources of this workbook flow from several streams. We have learned through our own efforts as congregational leaders. We have benefited from formal graduate studies and informal life lessons. As much as anything, we have learned from the faithful and effective leadership that we've observed in the congregations around us. We're grateful to all of the friends and family who have so generously shared with us. We want to be good stewards of their many contributions.

The Congregational Transformation Model

This workbook is based on the Congregational Transformation Model, which is shown in Figure 1. The model grew out of consulting and training with hundreds of churches and church leaders and from our research and study of leadership practices in Christian congregations and other organizations. The model is designed to describe a complex set of challenges, steps, and leadership requirements that are associated with a deep, systemic change effort in an established congregation. Its principles are also applicable to ministries within a church, a new church, judicatories, and parachurch organizations. The model has three major components: spiritual and relational vitality, four learning disciplines, and an eight-stage process for change.

Spiritual and relational vitality is the heart and energy source of the transformation process. Congregations without an adequate level of vitality will not be able to sustain the change process. A congregation that is not committed to following God or that is experiencing serious discord within the body will find it virtually impossible to stay on the path of transformation.

The learning disciplines are essential for leading transformation. Transformation requires a set of skills that are different from those that many pastors possess and that many congregations practice. Transformation does not require that all of the learning disciplines be mastered from the outset, but steady growth along this dimension is critical.

FIGURE 1   Congregational Transformation Model

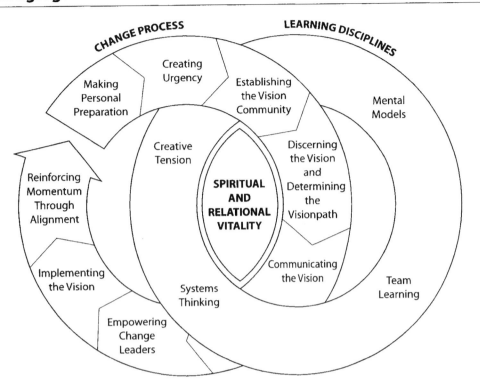

The eight-stage change process is the sequential component of the model that gives form and direction to the transformation. It is not enough to know that change is needed, to have a strong leader, or even to have a clear image of the church's future. The challenge is to create a realistic way to get there. The eight stages give structure and sequence to the process of moving from today's reality to tomorrow's vision.

There is no shortcut for leading congregational change. We do not offer a formula or a program. The model does, however, provide leaders with a framework for assessing and guiding transformation. The workbook is organized around the individual elements of the model. Part One explores the issues of vitality and the learning disciplines that are needed throughout the transformation journey. Part Two follows the eight stages of the change process.

How to Use This Workbook

This workbook may be used in a variety of formats. In most cases, a group of staff and lay leaders will use the workbook to guide their collective efforts to follow God's transformational direction. Often the pastor or other key leaders will have read *Leading Congregational Change*. In some cases, a pastor or church consultant will use the workbook as a resource in personal efforts to initiate and guide change. Once a reader becomes familiar with the contents, the workbook is designed to allow for easy adaptation to fit a wide range of congregational needs and circumstances.

Each chapter begins with a brief description of the topic. (More detailed descriptions are provided in the companion book.) Leaders are then invited to practice the topic through suggested actions to foster change. Some of the suggested actions are contemplative. Others involve gathering and assessing information for important decisions or help form critical skills. Still others will help guide the congregation through specific aspects of transformation. In addition to the suggested actions, we list resources for additional study of the topic and identify biblical passages that relate to the chapter's focus. Resources A through E provide other tools for congregational assessment and learning.

Part One: Vitality and Learning Disciplines

From our own experience, we know that the temptation to plunge into the change process is great. Part One is designed to put some judicious brakes on this urge. As we have already said, spiritual and relational vitality is the heart of transformation, and a new set of learning disciplines is needed to guide the process. With these five chapters at the beginning of the workbook, we hope to encourage congregational leaders to consider and cultivate their readiness for transformation before beginning the journey.

It is not necessary for the pastor or congregational leaders to work through these chapters in order. The important message is that vitality and the learning disciplines are integrated with and supportive of the entire transformation. One pragmatic approach is for one or two leaders to become familiar with the principles in Part One, and then to make suggestions of when and how to use this material. The activities in each chapter, which are both personal and corporate, are designed to facilitate this assessment.

Part Two: The Eight-Stage Change Process

The eight-stage change process makes up the second half of the workbook. We have found this approach to transformation to be applicable across a wide variety of congregations. These include differences in size, denomination, ethnicity, and polity.

Unlike the chapters in Part One, these chapters present a specific sequence in the stages of the change process. Congregations that follow these stages will minimize the pitfalls and increase the viability and impact of transformation. As leaders will see and experience, some overlap between stages is inevitable. But skipping a stage or starting too soon can have serious consequences.

Most of the activities in Part Two are intended to be done in group settings. As we note in Chapter Eight, a congregational leadership team called a *vision community* should be actively involved throughout the change process. Most of the activities in Part Two are designed primarily with this group in mind.

Timing and Sequence

Inevitably, we are asked how long it takes to transform a congregation. We always reply that there is no simple answer. We know that the transformation of an existing congregation is never a quick or easy process. But the actual time that is required will depend on many factors, including the scale of the change needed, church size, the congregation's readiness to transform, its spiritual and relational vitality, and past problems that may have been mishandled. Likewise, various stages in the change process will take different amounts of time.

In general, we find comprehensive transformation to be a five- to seven-year process, sometimes longer. Examples of comprehensive transformations would be a shift to ministries that target unchurched persons, a major transition in the racial or ethnic composition of the membership, movement to a significantly different size, or the journey from a "chaplaincy" stance to a missional posture.

We also find that the most effective transformational leaders master the *art* of leadership. They know when a congregation is ready to move forward and they provide the right style of encouragement. They recognize when it is time to slow down, regardless of the timeline that may have been set. The steps and activities in this workbook cannot be taken as a rigid formula. Leaders will need to sense when to spend extra time on a stage and when to move ahead. In the same way, we encourage congregational leaders to be attentive to when and how the learning disciplines from Part One should be integrated into the process.

If you do not consider yourself to be a *transformational leader* or if you become frustrated with this type of uncertainty, do not give up. The steps in this workbook are designed to help you. But we also encourage patience with a process that is always "messy." Even more, we highly recommend that the leadership responsibility be shared with others who can provide important input to these difficult questions.

Our conviction is that all congregations need to participate in God's ongoing transformation whether they're young or old, large or small, traditional or innovative. We believe that the model and methods described will prove useful to church leaders of virtually every heritage and style as long as they are open to learning and change. The statement at the beginning of this chapter was actually incomplete. In its entirety, it is not a statement but a question for all leaders to ponder: *If you keep doing what you've been doing, you'll keep getting what you've been getting. Can you live with that?*

We offer what we've learned with a spirit of hopefulness and confidence that the Source of transformation is ever ready to guide and to empower those who are willing and able to follow. "No eye has seen, no ear has heard, no mind has conceived, what God has prepared for those who love him" (1 Corinthians 2:9).

Leading Congregational Change Workbook

Part One

Vitality and Learning Disciplines

Chapter 1

Spiritual and Relational Vitality
The Driving Force of Transformational Change

> Spiritual and relational vitality is the life-giving power that faithful people experience together as they passionately pursue God's vision for their lives.

ALL OF US long to experience the power of spiritual and relational vitality in our lives and our congregations. In fact, this vitality provides the energy for congregational transformation. Unfortunately, many have given up hope of living with this spirit.

Spiritual and relational vitality are two dimensions of a single reality—a consistent teaching of Scripture. Jesus summed it up in this way. "One of them, an expert in the Law, tested him with this question: 'Teacher, which is the greatest commandment in the Law?' Jesus replied: 'Love the Lord your God with all your heart and with all your soul and with all your mind. This is the first and greatest commandment. And the second is like it: 'Love your neighbor as yourself. All the Law and the Prophets hang on these two commandments'" (Matthew 22:35–40).

All of the Law and the Prophets are summarized by a commandment to love God *(spiritual vitality)* and to love our neighbor *(relational vitality)*. It's like two sides to the same coin. Unconditional love for our neighbors is impossible unless we have a deep sense of the presence and power of God in our lives. The strongest indicator that our love for God is pure and obedient is when it results in a more faithful and effective expression of love for others. When we get out of balance, we are less able to influence the world in which we live.

The process described in Figure 1.1 is built on a fundamental assumption that God's people are called to live as an authentic New Testament community like the one described in Acts 2:42–47. When we do so, the church becomes "salt and light" to the world. In John 17:23, Jesus prays,

"May they be brought to complete unity to let the world know that you sent me and have loved them, even as you have loved me." Spiritual and relational vitality is profoundly personal and corporate. It pervades all of our attitudes and our actions. It must be simultaneously routine and revolutionary.

Spiritual and relational vitality follows the movement from an individual's encounter with God to the experience of grace, unity, and community. However, as the arrows in Figure 1.1 show, the flow of influence moves both ways at the same time. The experience of God's presence through Christian community leads to a spirit of unity and grace and a hunger for God.

When spiritual vitality is high, the congregation should experience a sense of healthy discontent, like people on a journey toward God's ideal that is always before them. Leaders and members alike should feel the Holy Spirit nudging them out of their comfort zones. They will be increasingly dissatisfied with maintaining the status quo. This provides a vital motivation and direction for transformation.

Relational vitality is a counterbalance to the stresses caused by change. Without relational vitality, disagreements over the change process can be fueled by distrust and by failures to recognize each person's unique contributions to the body.

Individual change leaders and congregations sometimes overestimate their church's level of vitality. Allowing the Holy Spirit to foster a strong sense of spiritual and relational health takes time. In a world of instant results, we want a process in which everything happens quickly. We pray a cursory prayer at the beginning of a meeting, engage the process with all

FIGURE 1.1   Elements of Spiritual and Relational Vitality

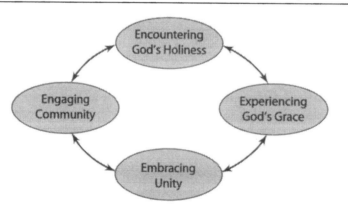

of our personal baggage, and ask God to bless us once we've decided what we want to do. Authentic spiritual and relational vitality not only empowers a local body of Christ, it prepares a church to become God's instrument in the world. As the challenges of change increase, so does the demand for this well-spring of power.

Suggested Actions to Foster Change

ACTIVITY 1-A   **Bible Study and Reflection**

Objective   To discern how our personal and congregational practices align with biblical descriptions of the early church.

Process   Reflect on the story of the early church, as recorded in Acts, and on your experience with God's transforming power.

1. What are the common patterns of God's movement in the early church? How did the church respond?

2. Identify specific ways in which God has transformed your life and your congregation.

3. In what specific ways at this time are you resisting God's desire to make changes in your life? In the life of your congregation?

4. What will you do personally to experience God's direction in your life more fully?

5. What does your congregation need to do to experience the vitality described in Acts?

ACTIVITY 1-B   ## Assessment of Spiritual and Relational Vitality

Objective   To determine the congregation's overall vitality and its readiness to move forward in the transformation process.

Process   Consider the following questions:

1. What is the overall level of spiritual and relational vitality in the congregation today?

2. How does the level of vitality differ in each of the four areas depicted in Figure 1.1?

3. Are there specific unresolved issues that create disunity among church members?

4. What specific actions will be taken to increase the congregation's overall vitality?

5. Given that transformation is a difficult and long-term process, does the congregation have sufficient spiritual and relational vitality to sustain this type of effort?

Note: Additional assessment activities in Chapter Seven can provide further insight into a congregation's spiritual and relational vitality.

Additional Suggestions to Build Spiritual and Relational Vitality

The Holy Spirit is the source of spiritual and relational vitality, and congregations cannot control how or when the Spirit moves. The church, however, needs to be prepared to respond and should seek ways to foster vitality. The following activities can create an environment in which vitality can develop:

- Convene a personal or group retreat focused on spiritual growth. Worship, prayer, Bible study, and quiet times should be the primary activities. (If the retreat has a planning or "event" agenda, it is less likely to foster spiritual vitality.)

- Create study groups using *The Divine Conspiracy: Discovering Our Hidden Life in God* by Willard (1998) or *Experiencing God: Knowing and Doing the Will of God* by Blackaby and King (1990). The combination of small group experience and the impact of a call to holy living can be a particularly powerful tool for stimulating vitality.

- Conduct a service of reconciliation, particularly for congregations that have suffered from a major conflict or from the moral failure of a key leader.

- Provide ongoing education and emphasis on spiritual disciplines.

Resources

Blackaby, H. T., and King, C. V. *Experiencing God: Knowing and Doing the Will of God.* Nashville: Broadman and Holman, 1990.

Clapp, R. *A Peculiar People: The Church as Culture in a Post-Christian Society.* Downers Grove, Ill.: InterVarsity Press, 1996.

Hunsberger, G. R., and Van Gelder, C. (eds.). *The Church Between Gospel and Culture: The Emerging Mission in North America.* Grand Rapids, Mich.: Eerdmans, 1996.

Sande, K. *The Peacemaker: A Biblical Guide to Resolving Personal Conflict.* (2nd ed.) Grand Rapids, Mich.: Baker, 1997.

Steinke, P. L. *Healthy Congregations.* Bethesda, Md.: Alban Institute, 1996.

Willard, D. *The Divine Conspiracy: Rediscovering Our Hidden Life in God.* New York: HarperCollins, 1998.

Chapter 2

Discipline One: Generating and Sustaining Creative Tension

Creative tension is the discipline exercised by leaders and congregations when they generate and sustain a constructive gap between current reality and a vision of the future.

GENERATING AND sustaining creative tension is an essential driving force for personal and congregational transformation. Creative tension is *generated* by contrasting a clear picture of how things are today (current reality) with a compelling vision of God's desired future. It creates discontent with the status quo.

Sustaining this tension is just as important, and just as difficult, as generating it. Human nature urges individuals and groups to reduce creative tension. We can do this by making progress toward the vision, distorting the view of current reality, or compromising the vision. Any of these will provide relief from the tension, but only the first response stimulates transformation. Change efforts fail, in part, because the leaders do not sustain creative tension long enough or sharply enough to allow learning and change to take place. Without sufficient tension, transformation is unlikely to occur.

Jesus was the master at this. He compared the righteousness of the Pharisees (current reality) to the righteousness of the Kingdom (vision) (Matthew 5:20). He told stories about God's reign that stood in stark contrast to the realities of the world.

The creative tensions experienced by change leaders and practiced by congregations are mutually reinforcing. Effective leaders learn to distinguish between tension that is creative and tension that is destructive. They resist the temptation to reduce tension too soon but also recognize when the level of tension is too high. In doing so, they collaborate with God's transforming movement.

Suggested Actions to Foster Change

ACTIVITY 2-A   ### Assessing Personal Tendencies in Dealing with Tension

Objective   To become more aware of how you normally deal with the tension between current reality and vision.

Process   Make a list of the last several instances in which you were challenged to learn or do something unfamiliar or difficult.

1. What were your feelings?

2. How did you respond? Why?

3. Was your response to those cases typical? Why or why not?

4. What do these responses suggest that you need to do differently to increase your capacity to generate and sustain creative tension?

Ask a trusted friend, peer, or mentor to give you feedback on your assessment and plans.

ACTIVITY 2-B   ### Setting Meaningful Goals

Objective   To develop goals that provide direction and motivation for yourself or a group.

Process   This activity will often be done in conjunction with Activity 6-D (personal mission), Activities 12-A and 12-B (change implementation), or Activity 4-D (team building). Identify something in your life or in the congregation's transformation process that is clearly a priority, like developing more faithful disciples or strengthening relationships among the members. Develop one to three concrete goals for this priority by addressing the following questions:

1. What are some specific attributes that are associated with this general priority?

2. Develop one to three goals for the priority using the following guidelines:

   - State them as positive outcomes (what you want) rather than avoidance statements (what you don't want).

   - Describe the goals using specific language that anyone can understand.

   - Determine exactly how you will measure whether the goals have been achieved.

   - Confirm that the goal is something under your control. If not, reshape the goal.

   - Assess whether accomplishing the goal is appropriate regardless of the setting. Note any qualifications.

   - Describe specific attitudes you will have to change or actions you will have to take to achieve the goal. Commit to making those changes.

   - Identify the implications of achieving the goal for other persons. Consider whether the goals should be reshaped.

ACTIVITY 2-C   Leader's Capacity to Sustain Creative Tension

Objective   To assess your own capability to lead a group to sustain creative tension.

Process   Creative tension always causes a certain level of discomfort. Sustaining creative tension in your personal life is different from leading a group to sustain the tension. Reflect on the following:

1. In current or past leadership roles, describe specifically how you have generated creative tension for a group by encouraging a clear assessment of current reality and shaping a compelling vision.

2. What biases or tendencies do you have when group members express discomfort? How do you answer when someone says that you're too harsh in your assessment; when someone says that the vision is unrealistic or unachievable?

3. Given that leaders need to be able to sustain creative tension, what will you do to improve your leadership capabilities in this area?

Share your reflections with a friend or member of your group and ask for that person's assessment, encouragement, and support.

ACTIVITY 2-D   ## Congregational Response to Creative Tension

Objective   To understand the congregation's tendencies in responding to the tension between current reality and vision.

Process   Individuals and groups can respond to creative tension in one of three general ways: distort their perception of current reality, compromise the vision, or make real progress toward the vision. Identify several instances in which the congregation has recognized a clear gap between God's call and current reality. Then discuss the following:

1. Describe the situation.

2. How did the congregation respond? Which of the three general responses was predominant?

3. Was there a particular reason for this response in this specific case? Or is this response typical for the congregation?

4. What factors in the congregation's heritage may cause it to respond in this way?

5. What will you do to increase the congregation's capacity to sustain positive, creative tension so that the benefits of this discipline are realized?

Also see the activities in Chapter Six and Seven.

Resources

Covey, S. A. *The Seven Habits of Highly Successful People: Powerful Lessons in Personal Change.* New York: Simon & Schuster, 1989.

Quinn, R. E. *Deep Change: Discovering the Leader Within.* San Francisco: Jossey-Bass, 1996.

Senge, P. M. *The Fifth Discipline: The Art and Practice of the Learning Organization.* New York: Doubleday, 1990, esp. ch. 9.

Also see the resources listed in Chapters One, Six, and Seven.

Chapter 3

Discipline Two: Harnessing the Power of Mental Models

> Mental models are the images, assumptions, and stories we
> use to interpret our world and guide our actions.

EVERYONE HAS mental models. They are God's gift for enabling us to process the massive amounts of information that our brains receive and for converting it to useful knowledge. Mental models are synonymous with *paradigms*—our perceptions and assumptions about the ways things are and should be.

We have mental models for everything we have known. They include such wide-ranging images as our concepts of God, ministry, love, family, fun, friendships, and church buildings. They operate even beyond our awareness on a continual basis. We tend to think that our own perceptions and assumptions are normal and are shared by other reasonable people. Of course, each person's mental models are unique. We run into problems when we automatically assume that the perceptions of others are wrong just because they don't match our own.

A central skill in mastering mental models is *self-disclosure*—the capacity to understand our deep personal beliefs and biases and to know how our life experience shapes our worldview. This kind of self-understanding is essential because the quality of every decision we make and every action we take is influenced by the accuracy and appropriateness of the mental models on which they are based. The challenge of self-disclosure is particularly difficult for pastors whose vulnerability can invite criticism and hurt, as well as hope and healing.

Mental models are also a significant challenge for congregations. Most of the "way we do things" in churches is based on deeply embedded mental models. In many cases, however, these models are based on a reality that existed a generation ago. Table 3.1 illustrates how the historical mental models diverge from today's reality. Getting beneath the surface to recognize and adjust our paradigms is no small task. However, the rewards for improving our mental models can be enormous because they are the keys to our attitudes and actions.

Suggested Actions to Foster Change

ACTIVITY 3-A   ## Images of the Church

Objective   To acknowledge and discuss our understandings of the church.

Process   Write the following biblical metaphors for the church on a board in the room: the Kingdom of God, the new creation, the new humanity, the family of God, the shepherd and the flock, salt, and light (add others if you wish). Divide into groups of three to four people, and discuss the following questions:

1. Which of the metaphors best describes your desire for your congregation? Why?

2. Which is least attractive to you? Why?

TABLE 3.1   **Two Mental Models of the Church in American Culture**

Stable Institution and Context	Rapidly Changing Mission Field
Slow, predictable change	Rapid, discontinuous change
Shared values in church and community	Divergent values in church and community
Pastor as manager	Pastor as leader
Homogenous target audience	Diverse target audience
Stable strategy developed by denominations	Continuous adjustments made to strategy at local level
Programs developed by national denominational entities	Programs developed by many different organizations
Standardization of approaches	Customization of approaches

3. Which do you think best represents the current life of your church? Why?

4. What needs to happen to bring your congregation closer to your preferred image?

Reconvene as one group, and summarize your discussion together.

ACTIVITY 3-B

Recognizing Mental Models That Affect Our Congregation

Note: This activity is best undertaken after the group has engaged in learning more about *current reality* and about the congregation's external context. See Chapter Seven.

Objective   To identify the "buried" mental models that may no longer be accurate but that may still drive key decisions in the life of the congregation.

Process   Identify a major ministry or activity of the congregation, preferably one that has existed for many years. Discuss the following questions:

1. What is the purpose or objective of this ministry or activity?

2. When did it originate? When did it take on its current form?

3. What were some of the assumptions or understandings of the church's environment at that time? Be sure to distinguish assumptions about church members and unchurched people. Make a list of these assumptions on the left half of a marker board or flipchart.

4. Are these assumptions still valid today? If not, what is a more accurate description of the current ministry environment? List these on the right half of the board or chart.

5. What are the implications of this revised understanding for the ministry or activity?

6. Repeat this process for several other ministries or activities to see whether a set of common assumptions emerges. Do these have broader implications for the congregation as a whole?

Remember that the purpose of this activity is to identify and examine the underlying mental models—images, assumptions, and stories—and not to discuss the content of the ministries per se.

ACTIVITY 3-C   ## Ladder of Inference

Objective   To improve our understanding and use of mental models.

Process   The *ladder of inference* spells out the thought process that generally occurs between gathering information and taking action. It helps us become more aware of how we form opinions that are often based on minimal or faulty assumptions. In drawing inferences, we move quickly through several mental steps.

The Seven Steps of the Ladder of Inference

1. Note someone's words or actions.

2. Select data from that experience.

3. Interpret it in a way that makes sense to us.

4. Make additional assumptions based on our experience.

5. Draw conclusions that explain the other person's actions.

6. Add this to our general beliefs about how the world works.

7. Take actions based on our beliefs.

Remember an instance with other persons in which it subsequently became clear that your actions were based on inaccurate assumptions. Write a description of what occurred using the seven steps of the ladder of inference. Then discuss the following questions:

- What problems occurred in this situation?

- What difficulties can be caused when we use inferences?

- How can you use this process to improve your interactions with others and your processing of information?

Resources

Barker, J. A. *Future Edge: Discovering the New Paradigms of Success.* New York: Morrow, 1992.

Driver, J. *Images of the Church in Mission.* Scottsdale, Pa.: Herald Press, 1997.

Mead, L. B. *More Than Numbers: The Ways Churches Grow.* Bethesda, Md.: Alban Institute, 1993.

Senge, P. M. *The Fifth Discipline: The Art and Practice of the Learning Organization.* New York: Doubleday, 1990, esp. ch. 10.

Also see the resources listed in Chapter One.

Chapter 4

Discipline Three: Enabling Team Learning

> Team learning is the process of enabling a team to produce results far beyond its combined capabilities as individuals.

TEAM LEARNING is the process of changing a group's purpose from communicating and coordinating to learning. It is about taking individuals—with all of their gifts, experience, and education—and molding them together into a living unit that is capable of producing more than the sum of its respective parts. It is about creating a high degree of alignment in purpose, so that the team's collective energy is focused in a single direction.

Katzenbach and Smith (1993) define a *team* as "a small number of people with complementary skills who are committed to a common purpose, performance goals, and approach for which they hold themselves mutually accountable" (p. 45). Individuals who work on the same church staff or who are a part of the same vision community should bring a rich diversity of skills, spiritual gifts, life experiences, and worldviews. When the early church was in conflict over who was most influential, the apostle Paul made it clear that he planted, Apollos watered, and God gave the increase. Planting and watering are both necessary, and both Paul and Apollos contributed what they did best.

Yet that very diversity, which offers potential strength, often becomes a challenge. Many congregations have simply chosen not to embrace the challenge of diversity. It is easy to stress individualism at the expense of cooperation, to misuse power and authority and view submission as a weakness. We contend that forming teams when they're needed is a key learning discipline.

Team learning is necessary not because people always prefer working together but because many challenges we face are simply too great for individuals or collections of individuals to achieve them. Many people dislike working in teams because it requires extra communication, "inefficiency," and loss of autonomy. But teams are necessary for transformational congregations to reach their God-given calling.

In the church we often work in groups—church staffs, committees, task forces—but function and learn as individuals. Group members simply communicate and coordinate so they don't get on one another's turf. These are actually *working groups* rather than *teams*. For many aspects of church life, working groups are perfectly suitable. The distinction between a team and a working group is complicated further by the current fad of calling every church working group a team (Katzenbach and Smith, 1993).

Teams can be distinguished from working groups in two important ways. Teams have significant, shared performance goals. In a working group, each individual member is responsible for his or her own performance goals. For instance, in a church staff, the worship pastor, youth pastor, and small groups pastor may each have separate sets of goals. They meet regularly to coordinate calendars and communicate regarding potential conflicts, but they do not have any shared responsibility for results. In a true team, the goals can only be achieved through the mutual, cooperative efforts of the members.

Another distinction between a team and a working group is accountability. In a working group, each individual is responsible to a supervisor. In a team, each individual is responsible to the rest of the team. Accountability to a team is much more challenging. It requires a level of risk that many individuals are simply not willing to accept.

So why consider organizing your work in teams? There is one primary reason. Is the performance challenge you face so large that individual efforts or a working group cannot achieve it?

Suggested Actions to Foster Change

The activities in this chapter are focused on team building. We assume that the vision community (see Chapter Eight) should operate as a true team, and that teams are probably appropriate in other areas as well.

ACTIVITY 4-A   **Assessing Your Attitude Toward Teams**

Objective   To identify personal biases or experiences that may help or hinder your ability to lead or work in a team.

Process   This activity can be used to guide the reflections of individuals or groups. Consider using it as an early team-building dialogue for the vision community.

1. Based on the definition in this chapter, have you worked in a team before? Was your experience positive or negative?

2. What fears or concerns do you have about being part of a true team?

3. How do you respond to significant performance challenges? Do you attempt to be the superhero, give up, enlist others?

4. Are you aware of areas in the congregation where a team approach is needed? What will you do about this possibility?

5. What do these responses suggest about your attitude toward teams?

ACTIVITY 4-B   **Empathic Listening**

Objective   To increase the capacity of the participants to listen more effectively in order to strengthen team dialogue.

Process   Ask participants to form pairs. They will tell a story, taking turns as the designated speaker or listener. The listener may speak only to ask for clarification. The activity can be done in three rounds, or stories, in the following order:

- A simple description of a favorite activity (two to three minutes each)

- An important belief or conviction (four to five minutes each)

- A subject that reflects an emotional topic (five to seven minutes each)

After all three rounds are complete, each person should describe to the entire group what he or she learned—first about the process of talking and then about the process of listening in this way. The goal of the debriefing time is not to share the substance of the dialogue but awareness about sharing and listening generated by the experience.

ACTIVITY 4-C

Distinguishing Between Dialogue and Discussion

Note: In *discussion,* the focus is persuasion. People describe facts, analyses, and opinions to convince others of their views. The purpose is to influence the understanding of others so that they can form shared perceptions and make decisions. In *dialogue,* the focus is learning about people. Individuals share their perceptions, beliefs, feelings, and values with the group. Others are asked questions that encourage their disclosure as well.

Objective   To increase awareness of the characteristics and benefits of dialogue and discussion.

Process   Read the definitions of dialogue and discussion above. Then respond to the following questions on a board or poster paper with a column for each style.

1. Describe the key characteristics of dialogue and discussion.

2. Indicate examples of each style.

3. Describe when each style is more and less appropriate.

4. Suggest the benefits of dialogue and discussion.

5. Decide how your group will use an appropriate mix of both styles.

Most groups tend to overuse discussion and underuse dialogue. It is sometimes helpful for the facilitator or group leader to interrupt a conversation and explicitly say, "This is an issue where dialogue is needed."

ACTIVITY 4-D

Determining Where Teams Are Needed

Objective   To proactively and selectively apply the discipline of team learning in the congregation.

Process   Identify one or more ministries or areas in the life of the congregation where the use of teams may be needed. The leaders and key participants in this area should meet for an exploratory discussion. Review the definition of a team versus a working group. Remember, a team has a significant, shared performance goal that cannot be achieved by a working group. Then discuss the following questions.

1. How will the group's actions be different if the group works as a team?

2. What are the advantages and disadvantages of using a true team approach?

3. Is the group ready to commit to working together as a team?

4. If so, what specific performance goals should be set for this team? (See Activity 2-B.)

5. Who else should be added for the team to function at its fullest capacity?

6. What are the next steps the group needs to take to become a team and move toward the goal?

Resources

Cladis, G. *Leading the Team-Based Church: How Pastors and Church Staffs Can Grow Together into a Powerful Fellowship of Leaders.* San Francisco: Jossey-Bass, 1999.

Hawkins, T. R. *The Learning Congregation: A New Vision of Leadership.* Louisville, Ky.: Westminster/John Knox, 1997.

Katzenbach, J. R., and Smith, D. K. *The Wisdom of Teams: Creating the High-Performance Organization.* Boston: Harvard Business School Press, 1993.

Senge, P. M. *The Fifth Discipline: The Art and Practice of the Learning Organization.* New York: Doubleday, 1990, esp. ch. 12.

Also see the resources listed in Chapter Eight.

Chapter 5

Discipline Four: Practicing Systems Thinking

> The discipline of systems thinking deals with congregations as spiritual and human social systems that are complex, connected, and changing.

MANY "QUICK-FIX" solutions for struggling congregations are based on a perspective that the church is a "social machine." When congregations are treated in this manner, new people, programs, and purposes are routinely imported to replace the ones that are broken or worn out. Leaders become the mechanics who routinely "repair" the machine. Of course, churches are not mechanical devices, people are not replacement parts, and biblical purposes are not negotiable.

Congregations are alive! They require particular resources and conditions to grow and thrive. They are designed and called by God to live in distinctive ways that include a faithful relationship with Christ and a unified community of believers. Every congregation is called to a unique vision that the Holy Spirit empowers it to live.

Congregations are complex. Under the pressure of time constraints and the lure of security, we are tempted to create simple answers to complicated issues. The task is to deal with congregations as the elaborate bodies of Christ that they are by carefully learning their unique characteristics, patterns, and challenges.

Congregations, like people, have intricately connected structures that underlie countless component parts. Experienced church leaders are familiar with most of these parts, although they are often unaware of the nature and extent of the interactions. They may find it difficult to explain how and why certain situations arise in their congregations.

Resource D presents the Congregational Bodylife Model, which describes how the parts and subsystems of a church may be diagramed. It is also helpful to think of a congregation as a sphere with four layers. The two outer layers are made up of *events* like worship services and Bible studies and *trends* like changes in numerical growth and morale. The inner layers deal with *structure*—deeply embedded practices like how money is handled and how leaders are chosen—and *mental models*—assumptions concerning how things are and how they should be, like the meaning of grace and leadership. Though we spend most of our time and energy on the outer layers, the highest-leverage changes are experienced by transforming structure and mental models (Anderson and Johnson, 1997).

Congregations, with their natural drive to adapt and enhance survival, are constantly changing. But when mere survival replaces God-inspired transformation, a congregation must make deeper changes to remain faithful and effective. The discipline of systems thinking can dramatically improve leaders' abilities to understand their congregations and make high-leverage changes.

Suggested Actions to Foster Change

ACTIVITY 5-A   **Congregational Self-Assessment**

Objective   To develop a comprehensive, shared awareness of the status of the congregation.

Process   Use the Congregational Self-Assessment survey in Resource E to gather information about the congregation. This tool is based on the Congregational Bodylife Model described in Resource D and in the book. The survey can be given to the vision community, a broader group of leaders, or the entire congregation. After tabulating the results, consider the following questions.

1. What areas of your congregation seem to be strongest?

2. What areas seem to need the most attention at this time?

3. In what ways does the survey confirm or challenge your perceptions or those of most church members?

4. How will you communicate this information and your conclusions to the congregation?

ACTIVITY 5-B   ## Congregational Systems Analysis

Objective   To explore how the various parts of your congregation interact and influence one another.

Process   Building on awareness from the congregational self-assessment (Activity 5-A), use the Five Whys technique (Ross, 1994) to consider bodylife dynamics.

1. Review, as a group, the findings of the congregational self-assessment in a room with a large white board or wall space for writing.

2. Select a key area that seems to need attention, and write it on the board or piece of paper attached to the wall.

3. Ask *why* the area received a low rating. Identify and list four or five key factors that contribute to the circumstance or condition.

4. Then ask *why* again, and identify several contributing factors. Continue asking *why* and identifying factors for up to *five rounds*.

5. Repeat the process with other issues rated poorly and for areas with high ratings.

6. Look for common themes and recurring factors. How will other parts of the congregation benefit when you address the underlying areas that need attention?

Note: An important assumption of systems analysis is that a problem may actually be symptomatic of other issues. The best way to improve one area may be to change another area first.

ACTIVITY 5-C   ## High-Leverage Intervention

Objective   To develop a plan that will have positive, widespread impact throughout the congregation.

Process   This activity is designed to build on awareness generated by the Five Whys technique (Activity 5-B) or any other congregational systems diagnosis. It uses a *force field* analysis to identify the *high-leverage points* for making changes. High leverage refers to actions that have the most appropriate and most significant impact for a given level of effort. It is generally more effective to "tip the balance" in a situation by first decreasing the resisting forces and letting the supporting forces increase naturally. (Also see Chapter Twelve concerning change implementation.) Follow the steps listed below, summarizing your assessment in Exhibit 5.1.

1. Identify a change that the congregation needs to make. (This should be one of the underlying factors identified using the Five Whys technique.)

2. For any change, there will be sources of support and resistance, both current and potential. The sources may be individuals, groups of people (formal or informal groups or the entire congregation), structural patterns, mental models, resources, or other factors. Identify the sources for the desired change.

3. Summarize the key reason why each source is a factor in the desired change. The reasons may be the attitudes, feelings, or beliefs of the participants or the current status of a situation or resource.

4. Rate the strength or power that each source has in this decision.

5. Determine the importance of influencing each source.

6. Determine which sources you will attempt to influence and state specifically what you plan to do and who will do what.

7. Routinely update your assessment and modify your approach as necessary.

As an example, look at the idea of changing to home-based Bible study. Young adults (Group) may support this change because they prefer the intimacy of a home setting. The plan may be to begin the change by doing a pilot project with the group. A mental model resisting the change may be that "we always do Bible study on Sunday morning at the church." This may be a deeply held model that is critical to influence. The plan may be a series of communications that focus on the purpose of small group Bible study.

Resources

O'Connor, J., and McDermott, I. *The Art of Systems Thinking: Essential Skills for Creativity and Problem Solving.* San Francisco: HarperSanFrancisco, 1997.

Rendle, G. R. *Leading Change in the Congregation: Spiritual and Organizational Tools for Leaders.* Bethesda, Md.: Alban Institute, 1998.

Senge, P. M. *The Fifth Discipline: The Art and Practice of the Learning Organization.* New York: Doubleday, 1990.

EXHIBIT 5.1 High-Leverage Intervention Worksheet

Desired change: _____

Support for the Change						Resistance to the Change					
Source	Reason	Strength[a]	Priority[b]	Specific Plan	Source	Reason	Strength[a]	Priority[b]	Specific Plan
Individuals:					Individuals:				
Groups:					Groups:				
Structural patterns:					Structural patterns:				
Mental models:					Mental models:				
Resources:					Resources:				
Other:					Other				

[a]Rate as strong (S), moderate (M), or weak (W).

[b]Rate as critical (C), important (I), helpful (H), or unimportant (leave blank).

The Eight-Stage Change Process

Chapter 6

Stage 1: Making Personal Preparation

Making personal preparation means carving out the time and space to discern God's voice and direction for the leader's own ministry and for the congregation, and living with the tension that this creates.

BEFORE INVOLVING OTHERS in a major congregational transformation, leaders must spend time making sure that they are ready. The process is always long and complex. Leaders who are not experiencing God's transformation in their own lives will have difficulty discerning God's vision. They are unlikely to have the courage, conviction, and stamina to lead a church through significant change.

The time of personal preparation allows the pastor and other key leaders to get ready for the journey that lies ahead and become more open to hear God's voice. It prepares them to make specific personal and congregational changes that may be required. This is the time to deal with personal issues and motivations that might get in the way of the transformation, and to rest and recharge—both physically and mentally—before embarking on the journey.

Bible Study Suggestions

Matthew 4:1–11

Matthew 7:3–5

Matthew 26:36–44

Luke 4:42

Mark 6:45–46

Galatians 1:13–24

Discussion Questions

- What role does prayer and personal preparation play in Jesus' life?

- When is the right time to engage in preparation?

- Are there areas in my life or in my relationships with others where healing is needed before I can serve in the role to which God has called me?

- How will I prepare myself to help lead my congregation's transformation?

Suggested Actions to Foster Change

ACTIVITY 6-A   **Self-Assessment—Personal Issues**

Objective   To increase awareness of personal issues that may affect your capacity to play a key role in congregational transformation.

Process   Respond honestly and prayerfully to the following questions:

1. What patterns from my family of origin are affecting my ministry positively and negatively?

2. What significant shaping events in my own life have current consequences for how I minister and lead?

3. What is my relationship with the Lord? What do I need to deal with for it to become more vital?

4. What other significant changes are occurring in my life at this time and how are these affecting me?

5. What do I need to do to strengthen my family relationships at this time? What specific actions will I take?

6. Are there other relationships that are in need of reconciliation?

7. What do I need to do to become and remain more physically healthy?

8. What red flags, if any, about my current emotional status require some response? Are there issues that I am dealing with that would benefit from the support of a professional counselor?

ACTIVITY 6-B   ## Self-Assessment—Leadership Style

Objective   To increase awareness of factors that may help or hinder your capacity to lead faithfully and effectively.

Process   Respond honestly and prayerfully to the following questions:

1. How does my own stage in life and my spiritual journey influence my ministry and leadership?

2. Do I have a clear sense of God's vision for me? What do I need to do to clarify this vision? What are the implications of that vision for my leadership in the congregation?

3. What personal strengths tend to enhance my ability to lead change? What personal behaviors, when misused, tend to hinder my change leadership efforts?

4. What new information and skills do I need to learn to become a more effective change leader? What will I do about these needs?

Note: It is very difficult to assess one's own leadership without feedback from others. Ask several trusted friends who have observed you in leadership situations to describe your style honestly. Solicit feedback about your plan to change.

ACTIVITY 6-C   **Accountability Partnership**

Objective To establish a person or group with whom you will become mutually accountable to help each other achieve designated objectives.

Process Accountability partnerships can be formed in pairs or small groups. They involve significant commitment, personal disclosure, and care.

1. Prayerfully identify potential partners.

2. If necessary, spend time becoming better acquainted with potential partners. Progress to step 3 only when you are sure you can be open and honest with your partner(s).

3. Formally ask the selected individual(s) to enter into an accountability relationship.

4. With your partner(s), confirm the specific objectives and the arenas of accountability. These can be very broad or focused on a single specific issue.

5. Determine the means of meeting and sharing.

6. Identify when and how the partnership will end.

ACTIVITY 6-D   **Personal Mission Statement**

Objective To clarify succinctly your current sense of God's purpose for your life.

Process A number of resources are available for the development of personal mission statements, such as Maxwell's *Success Journey* (1997) and Covey's *Seven Habits of Highly Successful People* (1989). A simple process is described below.

1. List a key activity that you do that is important to you.

2. Ask yourself why do you it.

3. In response to this answer, ask why this is important to you.

4. Continue until you are describing a very deep level of belief and practice.

5. Do the same exercise with other important activities.

6. Note the similarities and themes at each of the deepest levels.

7. Use these reflections to generate a one-sentence statement of what you believe to be God's mission for your life.

8. Write this statement, and place it somewhere that will cause you to see it periodically and reflect on it.

See also the activities in Chapter Two.

Stage 1 Assessment Questions

1. Am I aware of the major forces in my life that shape my understanding of the church and my own discipleship?

2. Have I confessed and experienced forgiveness for any wrongdoing of which I'm aware?

3. Have I experienced reconciliation with persons from whom I've been alienated?

4. Am I ready to make changes in my life, or lead changes in my congregation, as the Lord directs?

5. Am I committed to exercising spiritual disciplines, and do I have a trusted circle of friends who will hold me accountable?

6. Have other leaders engaged in personal preparation for congregational transformation?

7. Does our congregation have a sufficient level of spiritual and relational vitality (see Chapter One) and an adequate mastery of the learning disciplines (see Chapters Two through Five) to move forward?

Resources

Foster, R. J. *Celebration of Discipline: The Path to Spiritual Growth.* (rev. ed.) New York: HarperCollins, 1988.

Shawchuck, N., and Heuser, R. *Leading the Congregation: Caring for Yourself While Serving Others.* Nashville, Tenn.: Abingdon Press, 1993.

Sledge, T. *Making Peace with Your Past.* Nashville, Tenn.: Broadman and Holman, 1991.

Willard, D. *The Divine Conspiracy: Rediscovering Our Hidden Life in God.* New York: HarperCollins, 1998.

Also see the resources listed in Chapters One, Two, and Seven.

Chapter 7

Stage 2: Creating Urgency

Creating urgency means generating energy for change by contrasting God's ideal for the church with an accurate perception of current reality.

URGENCY IS CREATED by a clear realization that the church is not living up to its God-given call. By human nature we strive for stability and contentment. As a result, many church leaders want to avoid this stage. But urgency is necessary. When the gap between current reality and God's expectations is made clear to the congregation, God uses it as a powerful driving force for the change process.

Urgency helps organizations accept change and challenge conventional wisdom. It is no wonder that so many churches seem unwilling to change—they lack any sense of urgency. When urgency is fostered, it should lead the members, and especially key leaders, to begin to ask, "What are we going to do now?" Implicit in this is the recognition that the status quo is not acceptable.

Urgency should lead to an increased openness to God and a greater willingness to change. The creation of urgency typically has other consequences that many congregational leaders would prefer to avoid—conflict, denial, and resignation. Wise leaders understand that some resistance is inevitable, but they know that an accurate perception of reality is necessary for learning and growth. They find ways to strike the right balance between too much discomfort and a watered-down message that fails to build readiness for change.

Bible Study Suggestions

Luke 3:1–18

Acts 2:42–47

Revelation 3:14–22

Discussion Questions

- What are the defining characteristics of a vibrant congregation?
- If John the Baptist were in your congregation today, what would he say?
- What do the passages in Luke and Revelation teach us about portraying current reality?
- What other passages in the Bible form an important part of your understanding of God's mission for the church?
- What hope and encouragement does God offer your congregation, even if you perceive a wide gap between current reality and God's ideal?

Suggested Actions to Foster Change

ACTIVITY 7-A   **Raising Congregational Awareness and Sense of Urgency**

Objective   To stimulate congregational urgency for faithful and effective action.

Process   Begin to highlight the gaps between God's ideal and current reality for the congregation. The specific plan must be developed by each congregation. Remember to include both elements—God's ideal and current reality. Use worship services, sermons, teaching, training events, and written materials as a means of creating urgency. Generate enough tension to cause action without triggering despair. Stimulate urgency long enough to foster responsiveness but not so much that discouragement or resignation sets in. Be prepared to move forward whenever you sense that the time is right (see the Assessment Questions at the end of the chapter).

Note: The vision community is not enlisted until Stage 3. However, Activities 7-B and 7-C are particularly well suited for the vision community. Generally, these activities should be delayed until Stage 3, or the results should be reviewed with the vision community.

ACTIVITY 7-B   ## Understanding God's Ideal

Objective   To lead the congregation and vision community to a clearer understanding of God's ideal for the church.

Process   Use the following Bible passages, and others you may add, to clarify and affirm your church's understanding of God's purpose for the church.

Matthew 5:13–16	Acts 1:8	Ephesians 2:19–22
Matthew 16:15–19	Acts 2:42–47	Ephesians 4:11–16
Matthew 22:36–40	Acts 4:32–35	Colossians 3:15–17
Matthew 25:34–40	Romans 12:3–8	Hebrews 10:24–25
Matthew 28:18–20	1 Corinthians 12:12–31	1 Peter 2:9–10
John 13:34–35	Ephesians 1:22–23	1 John 4:19–21

ACTIVITY 7-C   ## Assessment of Current Reality

Objective   To develop a thorough description of current reality.

Process   Review the materials in Resource C. Decide which items to use, and gather the necessary information. (The results of the Congregational Self-Assessment survey, from Activity 5-A and Resource E, may also be used as a source of information for this activity.) Once the information has been collected, make advance copies for all members of the group to review. When the group meets, discuss the following questions:

1. What aspects of current reality seem to be most significant as your congregation looks to the future?

2. What facts were most surprising to you? Most disconcerting? Most pleasing?

3. What trends or common patterns do you observe?

4. Based on your assessment of current reality, do you believe that the congregation needs transformation? Is the congregation ready to move forward in the transformation process?

5. Are there specific issues that need to be dealt with immediately?

6. What information should be shared with the congregation and in what format?

7. Is there other information that needs to be gathered and assessed?

Stage 2 Assessment Questions

1. Have we developed a more accurate picture of current reality? Can it be explained clearly and concisely to others? (If it is too obscure or complicated for an outsider to comprehend, the message will probably be lost on many church members as well.)

2. Do key leaders in the congregation agree with the assessment of current reality?

3. Have we taken time to present this picture and its implications clearly to the congregation?

4. Has the message been balanced—not accusatory or "gloom and doom" but presenting "God-sized" challenges that can be achieved with God's direction and the cooperative efforts of the body of Christ?

5. As a result, are leaders and other members beginning to ask, "What are we going to do?"

6. Has there been a tendency to reduce the tension too quickly, that is, to reassure members that "everything will be OK" or "it's not as bad as it sounds"?

Resources

Ammerman, N. T., Carroll, J. W., Dudley, C. S., and McKinney, W. (eds.). *Studying Congregations: A New Handbook.* Nashville, Tenn.: Abingdon Press, 1998.

Bandy, T. G. *Moving off the Map: A Field Guide to Changing the Congregation.* Nashville, Tenn.: Abingdon Press, 1998.

Dennison, J. *City Reaching: On the Road to Community Transformation.* Pasadena, Calif.: William Carey Library, 1999.

Regele, M., and Schulz, M. *Death of the Church.* Grand Rapids, Mich.: Zondervan, 1995.

Schaller, L. E. *The Interventionist.* Nashville, Tenn.: Abingdon Press, 1997.

Also see the resources listed in Chapters One and Six.

Chapter 8

Stage 3: Establishing the Vision Community

The vision community is a diverse group of key members who become a committed and trusting community to lead the church in discerning and implementing God's vision.

THE *VISION COMMUNITY* is the core group, consisting of staff and lay leaders, who will be formally involved in the change process from the very beginning. They are critical in shaping, communicating, and implementing the vision. This does not diminish the role of the pastor in any way—it simply acknowledges that there are too many facets of change for one person to do it all.

The vision community focuses on discerning God's vision for the congregation. They should have a burning passion for seeking God's will and for helping the church to become all God intends it to be. They should also have the capacity and willingness to experience community together—to develop care and trust that will sustain them through the change process. This is not a committee or task force, terms that generally suggest "business as usual." Any name that causes this group's members or the congregation to misunderstand the importance and distinctiveness of its role is a mistake.

Who are the right individuals to serve on the vision community? Ultimately, this is a matter of prayer, careful consideration, and church polity. In some cases, an existing group (board of elders, deacons, session) may form the vision community. In most churches, however, this will be a newly created group. The first activity in this chapter is designed to help in this selection process.

The focus of Stage 3 is to enlist the vision community members and to begin building community. If the pastor or a small group of leaders are the only people who have been involved in the change process up to this point, Stage 3 is also the time to review some of the previous material and to provide necessary training. A retreat is an effective way to launch the vision community, since the setting and format can provide more time for building relationships. If a retreat is not feasible, the first several meetings of the group should emphasize prayer, community building, and training.

Bible Study Suggestions

Matthew 17:1–13

Luke 22:7–37

Discussion Questions

- The Transfiguration and the Last Supper are just two of the most notable times when Jesus worked with the twelve disciples to give them special instruction. Why did he do this?

- In what ways did Jesus build community among the disciples?

- What do the stories about Jesus and his disciples teach us about disagreements and diversity in a faith *community?*

- What are the implications for your vision community?

Suggested Actions to Foster Change

Note: Facilitation of vision community meetings is a key skill, particularly in Stages 3 and 4. When possible, consider using an outside facilitator for this role.

ACTIVITY 8-A   ### Enlisting the Vision Community

Objective   To enlist a group that represents the entire congregation and that can provide effective leadership in the change process.

Process   The vision community can be enlisted in many different ways. Congregational policies or procedures for creating ad hoc groups should always be followed. As a general rule, the group's size should be limited to 10 percent of average attendance or twenty-five people, whichever is less.

1. Pray about the selection process. Ask for God's wisdom in identifying the right individuals.

2. Consider the following qualifications for vision community members: standing in the congregation (admiration and respect by other members), spiritual maturity, the ability to make a meaningful contribution to the process, and diversity reflective of the overall congregation. The first three are considered to be minimum requirements for membership. Diversity should be reflected in the final composition of the group. The vision community should also include adequate representation of ministerial staff.

3. Determine the categories that will ensure diversity and representative membership. These will be different for each congregation. Some typical categories include age, gender, tenure at the church, and key areas of involvement. If a divisive issue is anticipated, it may be the basis of another category. List the categories for your congregation.

4. Use Exhibit 8.1 to ensure that diversity is maintained as members are enlisted.

5. Be explicit about expectations and time requirements when asking people to serve. Irregular attendance at meetings can be detrimental.

Note: In small congregations (average attendance less than fifty), it is possible to do the work of the vision community through a series of open meetings for all interested members. Leaders should assess the advantages and disadvantages of this approach.

ACTIVITY 8-B   ## Community-Building Exercise

Objective   To develop deeper relationships among participants as they become more familiar with one another.

Process   Depending on the size of the group and the time available, ask participants to take turns answering questions such as the following. This can be done in small groups or with the entire vision community.

1. Describe the family in which you grew up.

2. What have been some of your life's high and low points?

3. Describe your spiritual journey.

4. What attracted you to this church and what keeps you active?

5. What most excites you about the possibilities of our church's future?

EXHIBIT 8.1 Vision Community Representation

Place a mark in the appropriate columns for each potential vision community member. Make sure that all key categories have appropriate representation.

Name	Age				Gender		Tenure			Other	
	20–34	35–49	50–64	65+	Male	Female	< 5 Years	5–15 Years	> 15 Years		

ACTIVITY 8-C   ## Training for New Vision Community Members

Objective   To provide an opportunity for members to understand the overall change process and any work that has already been done.

Process   The pastor and others who have been actively involved prior to establishing the vision community should review the efforts and learning that have already been achieved. From this they should summarize the information that is most important to present to the entire vision community. This might include

- Status of the congregation's spiritual and relational vitality
- Overall context for ministry in today's society
- Congregational Bodylife Model (Resource D)
- Congregational Transformation Model (Figure 1)
- Data and assessment from Stage 2 (Chapter Seven)
- Mental models (Chapter Three)
- Team learning (Chapter Four)

For best results, presentations should be interactive and should reinforce key points. It will be helpful for the vision community to thoroughly master the Congregational Transformation Model. Review and repetition can take place over several meetings to achieve this learning objective.

ACTIVITY 8-D   ## Style Preferences of Vision Community Members

Objective   To increase participants' self-awareness of their learning style preferences, typical styles of dealing with conflict, and spiritual gifts.

Process   If possible, engage an outside trainer-facilitator to administer, train, and apply insights from one of the available assessment tools. Consider using one tool for each of three categories:

1. Personal style inventory, such as Bi/Polar, DISC, or Myers-Briggs
2. Conflict style inventory, such as *Discover Your Conflict Management Style* (Leas, 1997)
3. Gift, skill, and interest inventory, such as Willow Creek Association's *Networking* resources

Be careful not to use the personality insights to pigeonhole anyone. Instead, these should help the group understand each person's strengths, preferences, and patterns of interacting with others. Also, recognize that each conflict style has appropriate and inappropriate uses, depending on the time and setting.

Stage 3 Assessment Questions

1. Does the membership of the vision community fairly represent the church at large, including all significant segments of the congregation?

2. Has the group become a community in terms of its care for each other, commitment to a common purpose, and collaborative spirit?

3. As the group begins to work together, can a complementary mix of skills be seen? Does each member make a significant contribution that would be missed if that member were absent? Have any skill deficiencies been addressed with the appropriate training?

4. Is there freedom to challenge and disagree in meetings, without fear of reprisal?

5. In its excitement to be about God's work, is there a willingness to make changes, experiment, and try new ideas?

6. Does the group display a real sense of energy, enthusiasm, and expectation about what God has in store for the congregation?

Resources

Carter, W. J. *Team Spirituality: A Guide for Staff and Church.* Nashville, Tenn.: Abingdon Press, 1997.

Katzenbach, J. R. *Teams at the Top: Unleashing the Potential of Both Teams and Leaders.* Cambridge, Mass.: Harvard Business School, 1997.

Phelps, J. *More Light, Less Heat: How Dialogue Can Transform Christian Conflicts into Growth.* San Francisco: Jossey-Bass, 1999.

Also see the resources listed in Chapter Four.

Chapter 9

Stage 4: Discerning the Vision and Determining the Visionpath

Discerning the vision and determining the visionpath mean understanding God's preferred future for the congregation and the implications for congregational life.

GOD HAS A vision that is distinct for every congregation at a particular time and place. An effective vision is a powerful motivator for the congregation. It must be broad enough to generate excitement but detailed enough to provide clear direction. That is why vision and visionpath are both important. *Vision* describes where God is leading the congregation in the next few years. Because vision should be memorable and motivating, it is relatively brief. The *visionpath* provides the details that help achieve the vision. It describes key priorities and goals—how the congregation will move toward the vision over the next one to two years.

In this stage of the change process, the congregation needs to discern God's mission, vision, and visionpath. These three are related but distinct elements that describe the direction in which God is leading the church. Figure 9.1 shows the definition and relation of each.

Much of our application focuses on vision and visionpath. Vision is a clear, shared, and compelling picture of the future to which God is calling the congregation. The vision must be clear for the leaders and members of the congregation to understand it and match their actions to it. Vision needs to become shared, so that all of the body is working in unison. A compelling vision motivates the church to action. Many vision statements become so academic that they fail to create the excitement and enthusiasm necessary for transformation. Any one of these characteristics

FIGURE 9.1 Mission, Vision, and Visionpath

	Mission	Vision	Visionpath
Definition	General description of God's eternal purpose for the church	Clear, shared, and compelling picture of the preferred future to which God is calling the congregation	More detailed description of the steps that will be taken to achieve the vision
Length	One or two sentences	Several sentences or paragraphs	Several pages
Time frame	Eternal	3 to 5 years	1 year
Key question	*For what purpose did God establish the church?*	*What is God's specific call for our congregation?*	*How will our congregation achieve God's vision?*
Necessary perspective	Bible	Mission Prayer Discernment Church's context Vision community	Mission & vision Current reality Bodylife (congregation as a system)

is difficult to achieve. To accomplish all three requires discernment of God's vision, persistence, and hard work.

Many efforts to develop a vision fail to generate meaningful change because the final description of God's preferred future is not comprehensive enough. A clear and concise vision statement needs to be accompanied by a more detailed visionpath. Whereas vision describes the big picture of where the church is going, the visionpath begins to fill in details of how the church will get there. It explains the meaning and implications of the vision. If the vision is several sentences or paragraphs in length, the visionpath may be several paragraphs or pages long.

Bible Study Suggestions

Exodus 3–4

Acts 8:26–40

Discussion Questions

- When God reveals a vision, does he provide all of the details or explanations that we might want?
- Does God still have a vision for individuals today? For congregations?
- Are there unique visions for specific individuals or congregations?

Suggested Actions to Foster Change

Note: The general process shown in Figure 9.2 should be followed for the discernment of mission, vision, and visionpath. The following activities provide additional explanation and suggestions for this process. The activities can be applied to mission, vision, and visionpath.

ACTIVITY 9-A   **Group Exercise for Discerning God's Vision for the Congregation**

Objective   To discern a clear, shared, and compelling perception of God's vision for the congregation's next few years.

Process   Use a board or poster paper to create two columns labeled "The Way It Is" and "God's Vision," as shown in Exhibit 9.1. Note that vision refers to three to five years in the future. Ask the group to fill in each column for important characteristics of the congregation's life. Some typical categories are shown in the table. Allow enough time for discussion of each point. There may be genuine differences on some points.

FIGURE 9.2   A Process for Discerning Mission, Vision, and Visionpath

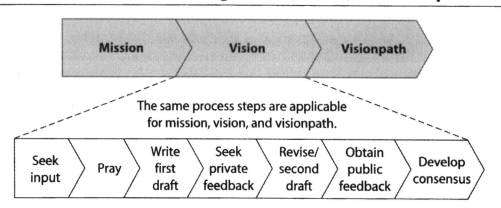

EXHIBIT 9.1   Contrasts in Important Congregational Characteristics

Congregational Characteristic	The Way It Is	God's Vision
Worship		
Discipleship		
Evangelism		
Spiritual vitality		
Relational vitality		
Care for one another		
Community impact		
Social service		
Prayer		
Confession		
Reconciliation		
Accountability		
Growth, maturity		
Other (specify)		

Leading Congregational Change Workbook, copyright © 2000 by James H. Furr, Mike Bonem, and Jim Herrington. Published by Jossey-Bass, San Francisco, CA.

ACTIVITY 9-B   **Drafting a Vision Statement**

Objective   To produce a first draft of the vision statement.

Process   This activity typically occurs after input is received from the vision community or perhaps the entire congregation. The actual drafting of the vision statement is generally done by a single individual, often the senior pastor. A significant block of uninterrupted time should be set aside. The writer should have the results of Activity 9-A and copies of all previously developed information (current reality assessment, vision community or congregational input, personal prayer journal). Before beginning, the writer should spend time reflecting on this information and in prayer. As pieces of the vision become clear, they should be put in writing. Typical elements of a complete vision description include

- The vision statement
- Reason for urgency
- Clarification of the needed changes
- Implications of the vision
- Call to commitment

The visionpath components will be added when they are developed.

ACTIVITY 9-C **Vision Statement Feedback and Revisions**

Objective To develop consensus around the vision statement through a process of feedback and revision.

Process Once the vision statement has been drafted and is ready for feedback, the vision community should meet to review and discuss the draft. A facilitator other than the primary author of the vision statement should be chosen. The facilitator should ask the group to answer four questions about the draft vision statement:

1. What is your overall reaction to the vision?
2. What questions about the meaning of the vision do you have?
3. Are there concepts or ideas that should be added or deleted?
4. Are there ways in which we can say this better?

The vision statement should be written on a flipchart or white board. As comments are made, the facilitator can use different colored markers to make changes in the statement. This process should continue until there is general consensus. The vision community should have a chance to "sleep on it" before considering the vision statement final. If the revision process takes several meetings, consider a second set of questions before adopting the vision statement:

1. Is the vision clear?
2. Is this a vision to which I am willing to commit myself?

When the pastor and vision community can answer both of these questions positively and enthusiastically, a solid foundation has been laid for the change process.

Note: At this point, or even before the first draft, the vision community may choose to engage the entire congregation in prayerful assessment and dialogue. Participants can express their perceptions of God's movement and calling.

ACTIVITY 9-D **Congregational Approval**

Objective To approve the vision and visionpath.

Process The pastor and vision community should work through the church's established procedures for approval of the vision. Ideally, this will include opportunities for presentation, discussion, and a final congregationwide vote on the vision document. Communication with the congregation is a critical part of this process and is discussed in the next chapter (Stage 5).

Stage 4 Assessment Questions

1. Is the final version of the vision statement consistent with the leaders' sense of God's mission and the particular circumstances of the church and community? Is it God's vision for your future?

2. Is the vision clear? When people read it for the first time, will they understand it?

3. Is the vision becoming widely shared by the members of the vision community?

4. Is it exciting? Do I want to be a part of this church? Will others want to be involved?

5. Does the visionpath provide enough detail to describe the congregation's future direction, guide decisions, and allocate limited resources?

6. Is there a strong consensus within the vision community?

Resources

Dietterich, I. "Discerning God's Vision Together." *Transformation*, 1997, 4(1), 1–14.

Morris, D. E., and Olsen, C. M. *Discerning God's Will Together: A Spiritual Practice for the Church.* Nashville, Tenn.: Upper Room, 1997.

Oswald, R. M., and Friedrich, R. E., Jr. *Discerning Your Congregation's Future.* Bethesda, Md.: Alban Institute, 1996.

Senge, P. M. *The Fifth Discipline: The Art and Practice of the Learning Organization.* New York: Doubleday, 1990, esp. ch. 11.

Also see the resources listed in Chapter Five.

Chapter 10

Stage 5: Communicating the Vision

Communicating the vision is a comprehensive, intentional, and ongoing set of activities that are undertaken to make the vision clear to the congregation.

THE CLEAREST AND most compelling vision is of no value unless the congregation hears and understands it. Communication is the critical link between the vision community and the congregation. We use the word *communication* in its broadest sense: engaging the congregation in dialogue in a variety of ways about the vision and its implications. Doing this is a constant task. Effective communication makes it clear that pursuit of God's vision is to be the congregation's singular priority.

In one respect, communication is an uninterrupted flow from vision discernment. But it also represents a major shift in the transformation journey. The fifth stage is where the vision and the overall change process become much more public. The implications of this shift should not be underestimated. Up to this point, much of the effort related to change has probably been done by the vision community. Communication has been done one-on-one and in the context of close relationships. The process has been intentionally structured in its pace, depth, and repetition to ensure that any miscommunication or misunderstanding is quickly resolved.

When the entire congregation is brought into the process in Stage 5, communication takes on an entirely different meaning. The communication stage should generate a high level of understanding and commitment to God's vision for the congregation. Failure to communicate the vision effectively can delay or even permanently damage the entire transformation process.

Effective communication blends creativity, repetition, and a strong awareness of the audience to deliver a message with maximum impact. Jesus was a master communicator. He taught his followers with parables, practical and patient explanations, Old Testament prophecies, and actions. He repeated his central themes over and over without using the same words. Christ knew that we would not fully grasp his message immediately upon hearing it, and we should strive to have the same patience and persistence with our audience.

Bible Study Suggestion

Matthew 5–7

Discussion Questions

- What are the different techniques that Jesus uses to communicate his message in the Sermon on the Mount?

- What messages or themes are repeated? How does he do this creatively without being repetitious?

- Why did Jesus continue to emphasize certain basic messages?

- What does this suggest about your communication strategy?

Suggested Actions to Foster Change

ACTIVITY 10-A **Communication Planning**

Objective To develop an explicit communication strategy that will build awareness and commitment to the vision.

Process Communication planning should be done throughout the change process, not just when the vision is first introduced. The Communication Planning Form (Exhibit 10.1) is a tool that the vision community or other change leaders can use explicitly to plan their communications. New plans should be developed periodically throughout the process. In using the form, leaders should ask

- What are the main messages we hope to communicate?

- Will our plan communicate this message effectively to the entire congregation?

EXHIBIT 10.1 **Communication Planning Form**

Date: _____

Key message(s) of communication: _____

Specific Steps[a]

Step (Description)	Target Audience	Responsibility	Target Date	Materials Needed
Small group meetings	Entire congregation	J. Smith (lead)	Sept. 30	Written vision statement

List of Communication Materials[b]

Material/Description	Quantity	Budget	Responsibility	Date Needed

[a]*Steps can be any range of activities: sermons, dramas, small group meetings, publication in newsletters.*

[b]*Materials might include written handouts, posters, videos.*

ACTIVITY 10-B   ## Small Group Meetings

Objective   To use a series of small group meetings for detailed communication of the vision.

Process   Small group meetings are a particularly effective but time intensive way to communicate information and obtain feedback from the congregation. They are often used during the initial introduction of the vision and at other critical (and potentially difficult) points in the change process.

Preparation for Small Group Meetings

1. Meeting logistics. Decide the location, time, and participants. If the entire congregation will be invited to participate, decide how they will be grouped.

2. Responsibility. Each meeting should have one person, preferably a vision community member (and often not a staff member), who will lead this presentation and discussion.

3. Content. Agree on key information to be presented and prepare any materials (handouts, posters) that will be needed.

4. Questions. Anticipate questions that are likely to be asked, particularly if controversial issues will be discussed.

Facilitation of the Meetings

1. The format should include introductory remarks by the vision community representative(s) followed by a time for comments and questions from the participants. The vision community member should conclude by summarizing key issues (positive and negative) that have been raised.

2. Introductory remarks should cover the purpose of the meeting, the format, and a brief presentation of the vision (or other message).

3. Take notes. If two vision community members attend, the one who is not leading or facilitating should make a list of comments and issues.

4. Avoid defensiveness if criticism arises.

5. Conclude by thanking the participants and telling them what the next steps will be.

6. Wrap up after the meeting by preparing a summary for the vision community to review.

ACTIVITY 10-C   **Communication Evaluation**

Objective   To determine whether vision communication is achieving its intended purposes.

Process   Periodically during vision community meetings, discuss the following:

1. Is the vision clear to our congregation? What actions by members give evidence that the vision is becoming more widely shared?

2. What questions or concerns about the vision are being raised?

3. Are certain groups being missed by the communication process?

4. What might we do to communicate more effectively?

Stage 5 Assessment Questions

1. Beyond the leaders, can a typical member of the congregation explain the vision to someone else? (*Note:* This is a more stringent test than reciting the vision statement.)

2. Can this same member explain his or her specific role in helping the congregation move toward the vision?

3. Has the congregation had sufficient opportunities to interact with and ask questions about the vision?

4. Has feedback been genuinely solicited, both formally and informally? Has the feedback been acted on?

5. Is there a growing pressure to begin implementing the vision? Is there evidence that people are beginning to apply the vision within their own lives and ministries?

Resources

Fairhurst, G. T., and Sarr, R. A. *The Art of Framing: Managing the Language of Leadership.* San Francisco: Jossey-Bass, 1996.

Miller, C. *The Empowered Communicator: Seven Keys to Unlocking an Audience.* Nashville, Tenn.: Broadman and Holman, 1994.

Also see the resources listed in Chapter Seven.

Chapter 11

Stage 6: Empowering Change Leaders

Empowering change leaders means cultivating a broader base of committed leaders and removing barriers that would prevent them from serving effectively.

TRANSFORMATION CANNOT occur without a broad base of committed leaders who are able to serve effectively. This requires developing and mobilizing leaders. In most congregations, it also requires making changes in "how things are done": organizational structure, job assignments, measurement systems, approval processes, budgets, and so forth. Without empowerment, congregations are unable to make adequate progress in the change process. Not only do these changes enable the process to move forward, they signal to the congregation the seriousness of the commitment to achieve transformation.

Empowerment consists of two equally important elements: (1) establishing a new model for leadership within the congregation and (2) removing the obstacles that would prevent leaders from serving effectively. Too many churches and church leaders attempt implementation without empowerment. That is why Stage 6 (empowerment) is shown before Stage 7 (implementation), even though the two are essentially concurrent. *Implementation* comprises the specific and visible actions taken to make the vision a reality. *Empowerment* is the set of enabling tasks that make these actions possible.

The new leadership model involves broadening the leadership base in the congregation beyond the pastor and a few lay leaders. This requires authorizing and trusting others to take on major responsibilities, and it often means adopting a new mindset in the calling and training of new leaders. In the past, the church may have simply asked people to fill slots on a static organization chart. When empowerment is taken seriously, leaders are affirmed by discerning the match between the ministry's needs and their unique skills, interests, experience, and sense of God's calling.

Empowerment is also about removing obstacles that these new leaders face. The more dramatic the change, the more obstacles will be encountered. The structures, processes, and rules that underlie how the church operates can be major barriers to change. These must be examined to determine where change-enabling modifications are needed. Both of these aspects of empowerment must be assessed and acted on for transformation to be effective. Change leaders will need to continually revisit empowerment as they move forward in implementation (Stage 7).

Bible Study Suggestions

Mark 2:13–17

Mark 6:7–13

Matthew 16:13–19

Matthew 20:25–28

Discussion Questions

- In what ways did Jesus empower his disciples?

- What risks did Jesus take in giving the disciples this much authority? What benefits resulted from his willingness to take these risks?

- In the calling of Levi (Mark 2:13–17), Jesus did not attempt to fix the corrupt tax collection system. Why not?

- How do these examples of empowerment apply to your church?

Suggested Actions to Foster Change

ACTIVITY 11-A ### Leadership Assessment

Objective   To assess which key areas of congregational life need more leaders and which leaders need additional training and support.

Process   Most churches do not have enough leaders. Discuss the following possible causes of the leadership gap in your congregation. Gather additional information as needed.

1. Does our congregation have members who are potential leaders but who are not serving?

2. Has the vision been communicated in ways that should excite potential leaders?

3. Is the church attempting to do too much and spreading its leaders too thin? Do some programs or ministries need to be canceled or reduced in scope? (It is better to do a few things well than many things in mediocre fashion.)

4. True leaders expect to have a certain degree of autonomy. Does the church discourage leaders by placing too many limitations or restrictions on them (not allowing them to lead)?

5. Would potential leaders be willing to serve if applicable training was provided?

The outcome of this discussion will suggest specific actions that need to be taken to cultivate more leaders.

ACTIVITY 11-B   ## Leadership Development

Objective   To provide targeted opportunities for developing more leaders in the congregation.

Process   Transformational congregations need to support and encourage their existing leaders and continue to train new leaders. What specific steps does your congregation need to take to improve its leadership development? Consider the following possible elements of a leadership development program:

- Monthly leaders gathering: Time for all the congregation's leaders to meet together for praise, prayer, testimony, and affirm the vision. This can be an effective time to encourage leaders, communicate important information, recognize important milestones, and facilitate alignment (see Stage 8).

- Leadership launch: Periodic event (for example, annual) focused on new leaders to provide initial training and communication.

- Mentoring: Pairing an experienced leader with a new leader (or apprentice) to create a hands-on learning environment.

- "Leader line" newsletter: Regular (for example, biweekly, monthly) letter from the pastor (or person in charge of lay leadership) focused on general communications, vision clarification, upcoming events, and celebration of achievements.

- Outside training: A variety of conferences and seminars are available for church staff and lay leaders to attend. The content of a high-quality event, and the time for the leadership team to be together (particularly if travel or overnight lodging is involved) can have many benefits.

- Leadership identification and matching process: A formal system with a specific individual in charge to continually cultivate potential leaders. This can avoid the inconsistent (and often tenure-based) systems that many churches informally use. Many resources are available to help match the gifts, skills, and interests of members with leadership roles.

ACTIVITY 11-C   **Organizational Assessment**

Objective   To remove barriers in the organizational structures and procedures that could hinder implementation of the vision and visionpath.

Process   Complete an overall assessment of the congregation's procedures and structures. The vision community should discuss the question "What aspects of our congregation's organization will be barriers to transformation?" Exhibit 11.1 can be used to guide this discussion. The entries in the exhibit should reflect the group's consensus, not just one person's opinion. The format of the exhibit will help the group see the contrast between the current and the ideal for their congregation. The organizational elements that represent significant barriers should be prioritized and specific plans for modifying them should be developed.

ACTIVITY 11-D   **Measurement Systems**

Objective   To measure the results that are most significant to the vision.

Process   The vision community should discuss the question "How will we know that our congregation is making progress toward the vision?" The answers to this question should suggest ways of measuring this progress. Often these measures will be different from those currently tracked by the congregation. Exhibit 11.2 provides a way to structure this discussion. Once a decision has been made, agree on how this information will be measured and reported.

Also see the activities and resources in Chapters Five and Twelve.

EXHIBIT 11.1   **Comparison of Current and Ideal Structure and Procedures**

Add other elements as needed. Place a mark to the left of the row if the element is a priority for short-term action. *Ideal* is defined as that which will be most consistent with and supportive of the vision.

Organizational Element	Current Status	Ideal Status	Benefits/Risks of Change	Specific Follow-Up
Job descriptions				
Organizational structure				
Committee system				
Decision-making process				
Budgeting				
Financial management				
Resource mobilization				
Communication				
Information management				

EXHIBIT 11.2 Defining Measurement Systems

Visionpath Element	Goal	What Should Be Measured?

Leading Congregational Change Workbook, copyright © 2000 by James H. Furr, Mike Bonem, and Jim Herrington. Published by Jossey-Bass, San Francisco, CA.

Stage 6 Assessment Questions

1. Does the congregation have an adequate pool of leaders to continue to pursue God's vision?

2. Is a process in place that regularly assesses the gifts, skills, and calling of members and matches them with needed leadership roles?

3. Are processes established routinely to train and support leaders?

4. Can the leaders who have been charged with implementation (Stage 7) do their jobs effectively?

5. Are their responsibilities clear and do they have sufficient autonomy?

6. Have significant barriers to implementation been identified and plans made to overcome them?

7. Are the congregation's ways of doing things beginning to change?

Resources

Center for Parish Development. *Organizational Concepts for Church Transformation.* Chicago: Center for Parish Development, 1993.

Hersey, P., Blanchard, K. H., and Johnson, D. E. *Management of Organizational Behavior: Utilizing Human Resources.* (7th ed.) Upper Saddle River, N.J.: Prentice Hall, 1996.

Maxwell, J. C. *Developing the Leaders Around You.* Nashville, Tenn.: Nelson, 1995.

Parsons, G., and Leas, S. B. *Understand Your Congregation as a System: The Manual.* Bethesda, Md.: Alban Institute, 1993.

Also see resources listed in Chapters Five, Twelve, and Thirteen.

Chapter 12

Stage 7: Implementing the Vision

> Implementing the vision is a specific set of coordinated, high-leverage actions that move the congregation toward realization of God's vision.

TRANSFORMATION DOES NOT occur just because God's vision has been discerned and communicated. Nor does it result from one simple set of changes. In fact, at the outset, it is impossible even to identify all the changes that will need to be made. In Stage 7, the congregation's leaders identify the highest-leverage actions that can be taken to move toward the vision. Plans must be developed to ensure that effective implementation follows. Change leaders also must continually assess the congregation's progress in the change journey and identify new high-leverage actions.

It is not a coincidence that the implementation stage occurs when the change process is three-fourths complete. Implementation cannot be done effectively any earlier in the process. Implementation requires the direction shown by vision, the support provided by the vision community, and the enabling of empowerment. Without these essential elements, implementation is just as likely to be the catalyst for major conflict as for major change.

Implementation should flow directly from the visionpath. It should be done in accordance with the priorities that have been agreed on by the vision community. Even though the specific actions will change over time, the church should continually be implementing new efforts to move closer to the vision.

Implementation is a single stage, but it is not a single activity. A helpful way to think about implementation and its relation to the vision is shown in Figure 12.1. Each level in the branched diagram—vision, vision-path, goals, and action plans—is more detailed than the prior level. Each is also directly related to the one before. Vision is the broadest and most general level. Visionpath is the next level of detail and generally has several branches from the vision. Goals describe the measurable results that are expected as the congregation follows the visionpath. Action plans are the tasks of implementation. They set forth the specific activities that will be undertaken to accomplish the visionpath and goals.

FIGURE 12.1 Relation Among Vision, Visionpath, Goals, and Action Plans

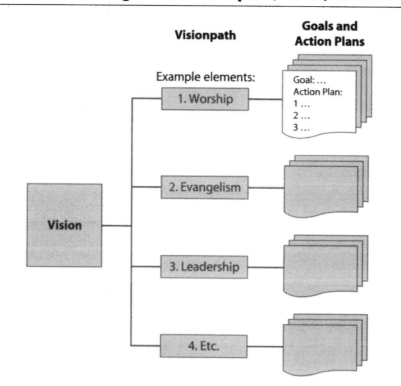

Bible Study Suggestion

Nehemiah 2:11–6:15

Discussion Questions

- God's vision for Nehemiah was the rebuilding of Jerusalem's walls. What were some of the specific action plans that grew out of that vision?

- In what ways and for what reasons was Nehemiah forced to modify his action plans during the course of the project?

- How did Nehemiah deal with opposition and setbacks?
- What principles about implementing radical transformation can you learn from the story of Nehemiah and apply to your congregation?

Suggested Actions to Foster Change

ACTIVITY 12-A   **Implementation Priorities**

Objective   To determine a set of high-leverage actions based on the vision and visionpath.

Process   Review the vision and visionpath and answer the following questions:

1. What priorities has the vision community already identified? These should flow directly from the vision and visionpath.

2. Brainstorm different action plans that could be used to achieve these priorities. A major action plan (such as devising a contemporary worship service or founding a crisis pregnancy ministry) is a significant undertaking that will involve a number of coordinated steps.

3. What specific action plans represent the highest leverage for the congregation?

4. How many new action plans should the congregation attempt to undertake at one time?

ACTIVITY 12-B   **Implementation Planning**

Objective   To develop specific plans to guide implementation.

Process   For each priority in the visionpath, more detailed action plans are usually appropriate to guide and communicate the steps that are being taken. Individual plans should be developed by the leader(s) who will be responsible for carrying them out. The plans should answer the following questions:

1. What specific steps and resources are needed to complete this action plan?

2. What is the expected completion date for this action plan?

3. Who has leadership responsibility for this action plan?

4. What specific, measurable goals are associated with this action plan?

Exhibit 12.1 can be used to formulate action plans. To check for completeness, go back and ask whether all the essential steps are listed (to the best of your knowledge). Have someone else review the plan and provide honest feedback.

EXHIBIT 12.1   Implementation Plans

Visionpath Priority	Goal	Action Plan	Responsibility	Target Completion Date

ACTIVITY 12-C ## Implementation Review

Objective To assess the progress of implementation and make changes as necessary.

Process The vision community or the team responsible for a specific action plan should periodically assess the implementation process. Questions to discuss in this review are the following:

1. Do we have enough feedback to assess this action plan accurately? If not, what should we do to get more information?

2. Are we on track versus the original plan? If not, what are the reasons?

3. Is this activity still helping our congregation move toward God's vision?

4. What have we learned that would lead us to do things differently? How should the plan be adjusted?

ACTIVITY 12-D ## Implementation Coordination

Objective To provide an easy-to-use summary of all implementation for the pastor and other key leaders.

Process This activity is most applicable for larger congregations that may have a number of concurrent implementation initiatives. Prepare a timeline with a separate row (line) for each major action plan (Figure 12.2). The left side should be a list of the initiatives, followed by a line that goes from the start to end date. Also label any major goals or milestones. The timeline should be updated periodically as plans are changed or completed or as new plans are added.

Note: The activities that are being performed in Stage 7 are closely related to those in other stages. In particular, refer to

- Assessment and reprioritization of action plans in Stage 8 (Activity 13-B)
- Empowerment in Stage 6
- Systems thinking (Chapter Five)

FIGURE 12.2   Timeline and Milestones for Implementation Plans

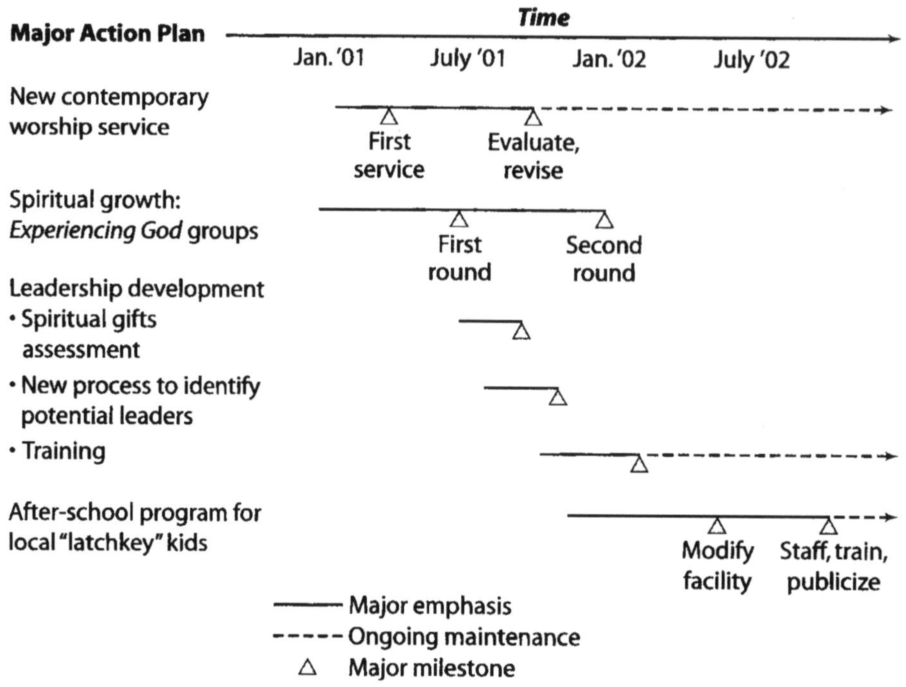

Stage 7 Assessment Questions

1. Have specific implementation plans been developed?

2. Have measures been established by which the action plans will be evaluated?

3. Are individuals in place to lead each action plan?

4. Have adequate resources been appropriated for each project?

5. Have the new initiatives been communicated clearly to the congregation, including showing how they relate to the vision?

Resources

Bass, D. C. (ed.). *Practicing Our Faith: A Way of Life for a Searching People.* San Francisco: Jossey-Bass, 1997.

Bridges, W. *Managing Transitions: Making the Most of Change.* Reading, Mass.: Addison-Wesley, 1991.

Shawchuck, N., and Heuser, R. *Managing the Congregation: Building Effective Systems to Serve People.* Nashville, Tenn.: Abingdon Press, 1996.

Also see resources listed in Chapters Five, Eleven, and Thirteen.

Chapter 13

Stage 8: Reinforcing Momentum Through Alignment

Reinforcing momentum through alignment means creating an environment in which commitment to God's vision is increasingly evident in all aspects of the congregation.

TRANSFORMATION REQUIRES that the people and ministries of the entire congregation be aligned with the vision. After an initial round of implementation, members will have a natural tendency to slip back and rest. Change leaders need to recognize this dynamic and continually revisit the vision. They need to celebrate the progress that has been made, but they also need to press ahead toward God's call. As they do so, new plans to increase the congregation's alignment with the vision should be developed.

Even with as much progress as the congregation has made to this point, the transformation is still very fragile. Alignment is evident when the majority of the people and ministries of the church are clearly committed to the vision. As alignment occurs, the change process spreads beyond a few high-leverage initiatives. The very culture of the church begins to change. A tangible sense of excitement, expectation, and everyone "rowing in one direction" will permeate the congregation.

The final stage of the change process is really not the end. As long as our world changes rapidly and God calls us to transformation, congregations will face continual change. So the eighth stage is not a conclusion to the change process but an ongoing effort to adjust to the call of God's vision and the world around us.

The need for continuous change goes against the grain of any organization. Even congregations that enthusiastically enter into the transformation process will inevitably ask, "How long will this process last?" They can become discouraged when they learn that a state of ongoing change needs to become their norm. But the evidence is clear and compelling that continuous adaptation is required. The good news is that the most difficult changes may well be those required in the beginning years of transformation. Every few years, the congregation's vision and visionpath will need to be freshly stated. A culture that embraces new opportunities and reaches out to a world in need can be created. And God will continue to guide and strengthen those congregations that follow his transformational call.

Bible Study Suggestion

Joshua 3:1–4:24

Discussion Questions

- In the language of congregational transformation how would you describe the crossing of the Jordan? Had the vision been achieved?

- What purpose did the stone monument serve?

- What does this story teach us about celebration of milestones and about ongoing implementation to follow God's vision?

Suggested Actions to Foster Change

Note: There will be an ongoing interaction between the activities in Stages 6, 7, and 8. Empowerment, implementation, and alignment are closely related parts of the change process. Furthermore, each of the activities in this stage can be repeated at regular intervals over the course of the change process.

ACTIVITY 13-A   ### Role of the Vision Community

Objective   To determine the vision community's role in the ongoing transformation process.

Process   The vision community is often established as an ad hoc group whose primary role is to lead in the discernment of God's vision and initial implementation. At this stage, its role usually needs to be redefined. Specific steps and issues to consider include the following:

1. Definition of the role (can range from disbanding to active governance). The most typical role is for the vision community to focus on specific issues that relate to ongoing implementation of the vision.

2. Definition of membership, including qualifications, rotation of members, length of term, number of members.

3. Anticipated meeting frequency.

4. Approval by the church or appropriate committee(s).

5. Enlistment or reenlistment of members.

6. Training and education for new members.

ACTIVITY 13-B   ## Assessing Progress Toward the Vision

Objective   To routinely monitor the implementation process and make adjustments as necessary.

Process   One of the major roles of the vision community is to monitor the overall progress toward the vision. The review of action plans in Stage 7 (Activity 12-C) is helpful input for this activity. The following questions can guide this discussion:

1. Are we making adequate progress toward the vision? Are we meeting our specific goals?

2. What do we need to consider doing differently?

3. What new action plans should we undertake?

4. What specific achievements or lessons should be reported to the entire congregation?

ACTIVITY 13-C   ## Communicating and Celebrating Progress

Objective   To keep the entire congregation well informed of the progress that is being made and recognize individuals or groups for their contributions.

Process Share written and verbal reports with the entire congregation on a regular basis so that progress can be celebrated and adjustments to the visionpath can be communicated. The Communication Planning Form (Exhibit 10.1) can be used to guide this activity. A list of all major goals or milestones can also be kept to help remind leaders when celebration might be appropriate.

ACTIVITY 13-D ## Alignment of Members with the Vision

Objective To assess the overall level of commitment that individual members have to the vision.

Process It is possible, particularly in a larger congregation, that commitment is not widely shared at this stage. The vision community should periodically assess the congregation's level of commitment—both breadth and depth—to the vision. Consider the following questions in this assessment:

1. Does the average church member (regular attender) understand the vision?

2. Is he or she excited about God's plans for the congregation?

3. As changes have been made, how much conflict has occurred? (Some conflict is normal, but extensive resistance is a sign of low commitment.)

4. Has it been easier or more difficult to get people to volunteer for new initiatives?

5. If commitment does not appear to be widely shared, why? (For example, communication, wording of the vision statement.)

6. What steps should be taken to build commitment?

ACTIVITY 13-E ## Alignment of Ministries with the Vision

Objective To increase the congregation's overall alignment with the vision so that all of its ministries are working together toward a common goal.

Process Initial implementation typically focuses on a few, high-leverage opportunities. To create alignment, the church needs to move beyond this starting point and involve all of the different congregational ministries. As other leaders begin to understand and own the vision, they will be willing and able to initiate changes within their areas of responsibility to increase alignment. Use Exhibit 13.1 to identify the ministries and administrative areas of the congregation for which alignment is important. For those in

EXHIBIT 13.1 **Congregational Alignment: Assessment and Plans**

Area/Ministry	Degree of Alignment/ Explanation	Leader's Commitment	Next Steps

Leading Congregational Change Workbook, copyright © 2000 by James H. Furr, Mike Bonem, and Jim Herrington. Published by Jossey-Bass, San Francisco, CA.

which alignment is low, agree on specific steps to increase alignment. These might include

- Additional training
- New leadership
- More direct staff involvement
- A challenge to set specific goals
- Evaluation of the ministry's activities in the context of the vision

ACTIVITY 13-F   **Ongoing Vision and Visionpath Modification**

Objective   To revisit and revise the vision and visionpath periodically to faithfully follow the Lord's movement and direction.

Process   Periodically (we recommend once a year), the vision community should refocus on the vision and visionpath. The purpose of this effort is to determine whether any changes need to be made in the vision statement or in how the vision is being followed. A retreat or extended meeting time is the best format. Suggestions for the agenda of this meeting include

1. Prior to the meeting, ask all vision community members to prayerfully consider what further changes, if any, God may be calling the congregation to make.

2. Begin the meeting with worship and prayer.

3. Review the major initiatives and accomplishments over the past year (or since the last major review).

4. Review the vision and visionpath. Allow members to express what it has come to mean to them personally.

5. Focus on the vision: Ask whether anyone has a sense that changes in the vision are needed.

6. Continue this discussion until there is clear consensus.

7. Focus on the visionpath: Ask whether the vision (as revised or affirmed) and current reality suggest changes in the visionpath. These may be restatements or updates to current priorities or they may be entirely new elements of the visionpath.

8. Discuss and agree on the highest-leverage actions that the vision community and congregation should focus on over the next year.

9. Decide how the outcomes of this meeting will be communicated with the congregation. This may include a "state of the church" message, celebration of progress, or formal approval of specific changes.

Stage 8 Assessment Questions

1. Is the vision still clear and is it still indicative of where God is leading our congregation?

2. Based on our understanding of God's intentions for this congregation, are we making adequate progress toward the vision?

3. Is there evidence of increasing alignment between the vision and the different ministries and organizational units of the congregation?

4. Has the future role of the vision community in the transformation process been clarified?

5. Recognizing that the change process is an ongoing, circular process, should certain stages be revisited? In some cases, urgency needs to be reintroduced. In others, it is time to revisit the vision in detail. In still others, the second half is the appropriate point of reentry.

6. Have we found ways to recognize and celebrate specific successes related to the vision?

7. Are we allowing opportunities for leaders and the congregation to pause and rest without losing important momentum?

Resources

Collins, J. C., and Porras, J. I. *Built to Last: Successful Habits of Visionary Companies.* New York: HarperBusiness, 1994.

The Ministry Toolbox. Computer planning software produced by Church Growth Resources. (See Resource A.)

Senge, P. M., and others. *The Dance of Change: The Challenges of Sustaining Momentum in Learning Organizations.* New York: Doubleday, 1999.

Warren, R. *The Purpose Driven Church.* Grand Rapids, Mich.: Zondervan, 1995.

Also see the resources listed in Chapters Five, Eleven, and Twelve.

Resource A

Resource Organizations

The organizations on this list constitute a diverse group of service providers dealing with church leadership and change. We recommend that you consider their premises and services before determining their alignment with your convictions and needs.

Organization	Books and Materials	Training and Conferences	Consultations	Facilitates Networks	Comments
Alban Institute 7315 Wisconsin Avenue, Suite 1250W Bethesda, MD 20814 www.alban.org	√	√	√		Established provider of many resources, primarily for mainline congregations.
Barna Research Group, Ltd. 5528 Everglades Street Ventura, CA 93003 (805) 658-8885 www.barna.org	√	√			Offers training and resources from an evangelical perspective.
Center for Parish Development 5407 South University Avenue Chicago, IL 60615 (312) 752-1596	√	√	√		Provides services for congregations and church bodies involved in transformation.
Church Growth Resources 15705 Bishop Street Cambridge, Ontario, Canada N1R 7J4 (519) 622-2262 www.ministrytoolbox.com	√	√			Produces training for the Ministry Toolbox church planning software.
Church Resource Ministries 1240 North Lakeview Avenue, Suite 120 Anaheim, CA 92807 (800) 777–6658 www.crmnet.org		√	√	√	Develops networks of church leaders for support and training.
ChurchSmart Resources 350 Randy Road, Suite 5 Carol Stream, IL 60188 (800) 253-4276 www.churchsmart.com	√	√			Distributes the Natural Church Development survey and resources and trains consultants to use them.
CitiReach International 5775 North Union Boulevard Colorado Springs, CO 80918 (719) 277-7925 www.citireach.org		√	√	√	Facilitates and encourages urban church leaders for the transformation of their cities.

Organization	Books and Materials	Training and Conferences	Consultations	Facilitates Networks	Comments
Denominational Church Renewal/ Growth/Development Departments					May provide a variety of resources.
Easum, Bandy and Associates 554 Bayside Dr. Port Aransas, TX 78373 (361) 749-5364 www.easumbandy.com	√	√	√		Training and consulting firm led by Bill Easum and Tom Bandy.
FaithSystems 9634 S. Kensington Dr. Houston, TX 77031 (281) 568-3303 www.faithsystems.com	√	√	√		Training and consulting network founded by James Furr.
Gospel and Our Culture Network 101 East Thirteenth Street Holland, MI 49423 (616) 392-8555 www.gocn.org	√	√		√	Network of mostly mainline church leaders working to define a vital new role for the church in North America.
INJOY P.O. Box 7700 Atlanta, GA 30357 (800) 333-6506 www.injoy.com	√	√	√		Organization founded by popular author and speaker John Maxwell.
Kingdom Transformation Partners P.O. Box 2272 Bellaire, TX 77402 (713) 838-9472		√	√		Specializes in congregational transformation and leadership development.
Leadership Network 2501 Cedar Springs LB-5, Suite 200 Dallas, TX 75201 (800) 765-5323 www.leadnet.org	√	√		√	Very broad network of church leaders attempting to build on "islands of health and wholeness."
Pegasus Communications, Inc. One Moody Street Waltham, MA 02453 (781) 398-9700 www.pegasuscom.com	√	√			Produces materials related to organizational learning and systems thinking.

Organization	Books and Materials	Training and Conferences	Consultations	Facilitates Networks	Comments
Percept 151 Kalmus Drive, Suite A104 Costa Mesa, CA 92626 (800) 442-6277 www.perceptnet.com	√	√	√		Provides wide variety of demographic resources for congregations and other groups.
Renovaire Eight Inverness Drive East, Suite 102 Englewood, CO 80112 (303) 792-1052	√	√		√	Fosters spiritual formation through conferences and other resources.
Saddleback Community Church One Saddleback Parkway Lake Forest, CA 92630 (949) 586-2000 www.saddleback.com/seminars	√	√		√	Resources and support for churches. Saddleback pastor, Rick Warren, is author of *The Purpose Driven Church.*
Willow Creek Association P.O. Box 3188 Barrington, IL 60011 (800) 570-9812 www.willowcreek.org/wca	√	√		√	Resource and support network for churches. Connected with Bill Hybels's Willow Creek Church near Chicago.

Resource B

An Annotated Bibliography of Useful Publications

Ammerman, N. T., Carroll, J. W., Dudley, C. S., and McKinney, W. (eds.). *Studying Congregations: A New Handbook*. Nashville, Tenn.: Abingdon Press, 1998.

A scholarly but accessible guide to conducting a comprehensive congregational study.

Bandy, T. G. *Moving off the Map: A Field Guide to Changing the Congregation*. Nashville, Tenn.: Abingdon Press, 1998.

Describes an insightful process by which church leaders can better understand their current situation and move toward God's vision for them.

Blackaby, H. T., and King, C. V. *Experiencing God: Knowing and Doing the Will of God*. Nashville, Tenn.: Broadman and Holman, 1990.

Uses a workbook format to help readers explore the depth of their willingness and calling to participate in God's movement in our world.

Cladis, G. *Leading the Team-Based Church: How Pastors and Church Staffs Can Grow Together into a Powerful Fellowship of Leaders*. San Francisco: Jossey-Bass, 1999.

A theologically grounded resource of practical strategies for helping groups become genuine teams.

Clapp, R. *A Peculiar People: The Church as Culture in a Post-Christian Society*. Downers Grove, Ill.: InterVarsity Press, 1996.

An extremely challenging call to practice Christian community in a powerful and prophetic manner.

Collins, J. C., and Porras, J. I. *Built to Last: Successful Habits of Visionary Companies*. New York: HarperBusiness, 1994.

Based on an exhaustive study of dozens of companies with long histories of success, the authors summarize the keys to organizations with enduring legacies.

Dennison, J. *City Reaching: On the Road to Community Transformation*. Pasadena, Calif.: William Carey Library, 1999.

The transformation of individual congregations may well converge with this powerful new movement that mobilizes "the whole church to reach a whole city with the whole gospel."

Hawkins, T. R. *The Learning Congregation: A New Vision of Leadership*. Louisville, Ky.: Westminster/John Knox, 1997.

An overview of how the concepts of learning organizations apply to congregations.

Hunsberger, G. R., and Van Gelder, C. (eds.). *The Church Between Gospel and Culture: The Emerging Mission in North America*. Grand Rapids, Mich.: Eerdmans, 1996.

A rich volume summoning the church in North America to abandon its historic coziness with culture and assert its distinctive missional character in our postmodern context.

Katzenbach, J. R., and Smith, D. K. *The Wisdom of Teams: Creating the High-Performance Organization*. Boston: Harvard Business School Press, 1993.

A classic treatment of the nature of high-performance teams and what it takes to become one.

Morris, D. E., and Olsen, C. M. *Discerning God's Will Together: A Spiritual Practice for the Church*. Nashville, Tenn.: Upper Room, 1997.

A guide for vision discernment that takes seriously the spiritual nature of the process.

Parsons, G., and Leas, S. B. *Understanding Your Congregation as a System: The Manual*. Bethesda, Md.: Alban Institute, 1993.

The authors provide a very useful approach to assessing and addressing seven of the most crucial systems of congregational life. The self-scoring inventories include basic interpretations; the manual explains the dynamics in more detail.

Quinn, R. E. *Deep Change: Discovering the Leader Within*. San Francisco: Jossey-Bass, 1996.

Challenges readers to embrace the necessary but most difficult aspect of leadership—personal transformation.

Rendle, G. R. *Leading Change in the Congregation: Spiritual and Organizational Tools for Leaders*. Bethesda, Md.: Alban Institute, 1998.

A pithy guide that offers lots of helpful tools for understanding and implementing change from an organizational systems perspective.

Schaller, L. E. *The Interventionist.* Nashville, Tenn.: Abingdon Press, 1997.

An exhaustive set of church diagnostic frameworks and questions from one of the most recognized veterans of church consulting.

Senge, P. M. *The Fifth Discipline: The Art and Practice of the Learning Organization.* New York: Doubleday, 1990.

The seminal publication that inaugurated a new level of emphasis on organizations of all types as learning organizations.

Senge, P. M., and others. *The Fifth Discipline Fieldbook: Strategies and Tools for Building a Learning Organization.* New York: Doubleday, 1994.

A virtual encyclopedia of insights and techniques for mastering the disciplines of the learning organization.

Shawchuck, N., and Heuser, R. *Managing the Congregation: Building Effective Systems to Serve People.* Nashville, Tenn.: Abingdon Press, 1996.

A comprehensive overview of how church leaders can use a systems approach to align their congregation in ways that achieve shared vision.

Steinke, P. L. *Healthy Congregations.* Bethesda, Md.: Alban Institute, 1996.

Applies the insights of family systems theory to congregational life, offering useful concepts and skills.

Warren, R. *The Purpose Driven Church.* Grand Rapids, Mich.: Zondervan, 1995.

An extremely readable volume about how Saddleback Church in California developed. Warren describes the power of a church that is highly aligned from purpose to parking lots.

Willard, D. *The Divine Conspiracy: Rediscovering Our Hidden Life in God.* New York: HarperCollins, 1998.

A profound work about living as a faithful disciple.

Questionnaires, Inventories, and Other Data-Gathering Resources

Information from the following sources can contribute to a more accurate assessment of the congregation's current reality:

- Church history timeline
- Church statistical history
- New member profile
- Church facilities assessment
- Membership residence map and demographics
- Membership questionnaire
- Community demographic information
- Community leader interviews
- Community resident interviews

Data-gathering forms and instructions are provided in this resource. Decide which sources will be used and who will obtain the information.

Additional information to gather and analyze might include

- Diagram of the congregation's organizational structure
- Summary of ministries and activities

- List of church organizations, committees, and groups and their leaders
- Official church documents (constitution, bylaws, policy manual)
- Written history of the congregation (if one exists)

Church History Timeline

The spiritual, relational, and organizational events in a church's past are crucial elements of the congregation's present. Some of these experiences are sources of great strength and merit continued celebration. Other situations may have been painful episodes for which healing is still not complete. Fully understanding and pursuing God's vision for the future requires a clear perception of this history. The Church History Timeline chart (Exhibit C.1) provides a way to summarize the most significant facts. Seven categories of information are included.

Year   If possible, start at the very beginning of the church's life—the period before its incorporation. If the church is very old, it is not necessary to include data for every year. Draw a line below each row of entries for a given year.

Organizational Developments   This category includes elements such as legal incorporation, land purchases, building projects, debt retirement, site relocations, and sharing of facilities with other groups.

Church Staff Changes   Note when senior pastors and other staff started and ended their ministries with the church and the primary reason for their departure.

Relationship with the Community   Some congregations begin as a church almost entirely of persons who live near the facility. Some have never drawn members heavily from the geographical neighborhood but have reached a specific group of people. Other congregations began by reaching nearby residents but now include a significant number who commute to the church from outlying areas. What has been the trend in your church? The years assigned to these developmental stages will probably be rough estimates. Also list any significant interactions with the community.

Major Ministries Started and Ended   List the starting date (and ending date, if applicable) of the major ministries of the church, such as worship, discipleship, and social services.

EXHIBIT C.1   Church History Timeline

Church _____

Prepared by _____   Date of Completion _____   Page _____

Year	Organizational Developments	Church Staff Changes	Relationship with the Community	Major Ministries Started/Ended	Changes in Spiritual or Relational Vitality	Other Significant Events or Developments

Changes in Spiritual or Relational Vitality   Were there distinctive times or events in which the church was especially responsive to God's leadership? When the congregation seemed clearly unresponsive to the Lord? When the people were particularly close and supportive of each other? When the church was involved in intense conflict? Note these things in this column.

Other Significant Events or Developments   List any other noteworthy aspects of the church's history that seem to fall outside of the other categories, such as sponsorship of a new church, development of a long-range plan, or demographic shifts in the community.

Church Statistical History

Complete the chart in Exhibit C.2. Customize the categories to fit your denominational heritage and congregation. Approximate if necessary.

New Member Profile

Exhibit C.3 provides a way to identify patterns among new members. In the left-hand column, list the name of each individual who has joined the church within the past three years or a good sample of new persons (family members will each be listed individually).

The next eight columns form four pairs to identify four areas of information: proximity (nearness to the church facility), ties (relationships with existing members), source (method of joining congregation), and activity (current involvement in church life). One column in each pair should be checked for each new member with the exception of the ties column. If the new member is not related by kinship or friendship, both columns will remain blank.

Proximity Columns

Check "Lives Near Church Facilities" if the new member lived in the neighborhood where the church facility is located at the time he or she joined the church. Confer with church staff and other leaders to determine what geographical area this constitutes. Think more in terms of where your ministries focus rather than where members live.

Ties Columns

Check the kinship column if the new member was related by family to a church member (child, spouse, nephew, cousin) when he or she joined. Check the friendship column if the new member already had a neighbor, friend, or business associate who was a church member. (This would not

EXHIBIT C.2 Church Statistical History

	15 Years Ago	10 Years Ago	Last 5 Years				
Resident membership							
Baptisms							
Resident membership divided by baptisms							
New members added by transfer							
Reductions in membership (death, transfer, other)							
Average Bible study attendance							
Average worship attendance							
Percentage of members involved in ministry							
New ministries started to target unchurched people							
New churches or missions started							
Total giving: general budget							
Total giving: designated							
Percentage of total budget spent on outreach, evangelism, missions							
Number of individuals participating in organized prayer ministry							
Average number of visitors per Sunday							
Other significant trends (specify)							

EXHIBIT C.3 New Member Profile

Period covered: From _____ to _____

Name[a]	Proximity		Ties		Source		Activity		Comments
	Lives Near Church Facilities	Does Not Live Near Facilities	Kinship Ties with Member(s)	Friendship Ties with Member(s)	Joined by Transfer or Statement	Joined by Conversion	Currently Active	Not Currently Active	

[a]One individual per line; list each family member separately.

apply to friendship ties established through a church outreach program over a relatively brief period.)

Source Columns

Check the "Joined by Conversion" column, if the member joined as a new believer making a commitment of faith; otherwise, check "Joined by Transfer or Statement."

Activity Columns

If the new member attends worship on a regular basis or is actively involved in some programs, events, or ministries of the church, check the "Currently Active" column; otherwise, check "Not Currently Active."

Church Facilities Assessment

Use Exhibit C.4 to conduct a thorough assessment of your church facilities.

Membership Residence Map and Demographics
Geographical Information

Obtain an enlarged map of the areas in which members of the church reside. Mark the locations of the residences of church members, using pins of various colors as indicated. Use one color for those who have joined during the last five years. Use a second color to mark the residences of active members who joined more than five years ago. Use a third color to mark the residences of inactive members. To indicate the residences of church leaders (define clearly who fits into this category), add a flag on the appropriate pin. (No individual should be represented by more than one pin.) However, if a particular residence houses both an active and an inactive member, two pins of different colors would be used.

A second option, if church membership records are computerized and if the congregation serves a relatively large area, is to determine the number of members in the four categories by ZIP code. This can be depicted in tabular or bar graph form. You can also write the numbers onto a map with the ZIP code boundaries clearly marked (and preferably with minor streets deleted). This will provide useful demographic data but without the detail of the other approach.

Other Demographics

Use the church membership database (for resident members) to identify other major demographic information and present it in either tabular or

EXHIBIT C.4   Church Facilities Assessment Form

	Superior	Adequate	Inadequate	Deplorable	Remarks
SANCTUARY					
Overall appearance					
Pews					
Pulpit furniture					
Sound system					
Acoustics					
Lighting					
Paint					
Floor covering					
Maintenance					
HALLS					
Stairs					
Lighting					
Paint					
Floor covering					
Maintenance					
RESTROOMS					
Fixtures					
Lighting					
Paint					
Floor covering					
Maintenance					
DEPARTMENTS, LARGE MEETING ROOMS					
Equipment					
Storage					
Lighting					
Paint					
Floor covering					
Maintenance					
Room size					
CLASSROOMS, SMALL MEETING ROOMS					
Equipment					
Lighting					
Paint					

EXHIBIT C.4   Church Facilities Assessment Form, continued

	Superior	Adequate	Inadequate	Deplorable	Remarks
Floor covering					
Maintenance					
Room size					
KITCHEN AND DINING ROOM					
Size					
Serving area					
Equipment					
Storage					
Paint					
Floor covering					
Maintenance					
Appliances					
UTILITIES					
Heating					
Air conditioning					
Plumbing					
Electrical					
OFFICE AND OTHER					
Equipment					
Storage					
Lighting					
Paint					
Floor covering					
Maintenance					
BUILDING EXTERIOR					
Overall appearance					
Paint					
Roof					
Windows and doors					
Steps					
GROUNDS					
Lawn					
Landscaping					
Sidewalks					
Maintenance					
Lighting					

Leading Congregational Change Workbook, copyright © 2000 by James H. Furr, Mike Bonem, and Jim Herrington. Published by Jossey-Bass, San Francisco, CA.

EXHIBIT C.4   Church Facilities Assessment Form, continued

	Superior	Adequate	Inadequate	Deplorable	Remarks
GROUNDS					
Parking					
SIGNS					
Welcoming visitors					
Basic information (church name, times)					
Leading to offices					
Directions for visitors (worship, classes)					
SERVICES FOR HANDICAPPED					
Convenient parking					
Ramps					
Access to sanctuary					
Bathroom facilities					

Leading Congregational Change Workbook, copyright © 2000 by James H. Furr, Mike Bonem, and Jim Herrington. Published by Jossey-Bass, San Francisco, CA.

graphical form. Categories that could be tabulated include age, marital status, and length of membership. Base data categories on the congregation's specific situation.

Membership Questionnaire

Surveying your membership with a written questionnaire can provide valuable information. Always administer a questionnaire in person, preferably just before or after a worship service, when you can get the best response. You may wish to design your own form or use the Congregational Self-Assessment (Resource E). Three other sources are listed below.

- *The Ministry Toolbox* is church-planning software that includes a huge member survey database and allows you to customize questions and tabulate the answers (see church Growth Resources in Resource A).

- The *Parish Profile Inventory* developed by the Hartford Seminary Center for Social and Religious Research is included in the book *Studying Congregations* (see Resources in Chapter Seven).

• The *Natural Church Development Survey* is described in *Natural Church Development* by Christian A. Schwarz and distributed by ChurchSmart Resources (see Resource A).

Another way of collecting information from members is through structured interviews. These "listening sessions" are best conducted by a qualified outside interviewer. They can be done with individuals or small groups and are thirty minutes to one hour in length. In the sessions, participants describe their perceptions, hopes, and concerns about the congregation.

Community Demographic Information

Detailed information about communities is available from the U.S. Census Bureau. To find the data center most convenient to you, use the Internet site *www.census.gov,* follow the links, and identify the state, city, or area of your choice. Several organizations market community demographic data. *Percept* provides information to churches and other organizations (see Resource A).

Community Leader Interviews

Make appointments with key persons who know about and relate to the community or communities served by the church. Following are types of people who might be particularly helpful:

Leader of a neighborhood organization

School principal or counselor

School board representative

City council representative

Commercial business owner or manager

Local pastor

Real estate agent

Bank official

Local social service worker

Law enforcement official

Day-care center director

These people can be identified with the help of a telephone directory, a community resource guide, or church members. It is important to select individuals who are *not* members of your congregation. In large cities, these people should be familiar with and focused on your specific community or communities.

Begin by explaining the purpose of the interview. Clearly define the community about which you desire information. Also confirm the amount of time that you will have.

Ask relatively broad questions, allowing the other person to do most of the talking. Ask follow-up questions for clarification if necessary. Take thorough notes. Do not commit the church to any specific response. Also, do not become defensive or argumentative. Be sure to ask for printed information that the person believes would be helpful in understanding the community and its concerns.

Leave on time unless the person invites you to stay longer. Before you leave, determine how to contact the person if you have more questions. Be sure she or he knows how to contact you. Send a thank you note on behalf of the church expressing appreciation for the person's time and interest. Write your overall impressions as soon as possible after the interview, while the information is still fresh in your mind.

Possible Questions

1. How do you serve people who live in this area? Is there a specific subset of the overall population that you serve?

2. How has the area changed over the last three to five years?

3. What are people who live in this area most concerned about?

4. What do you think people who live in this area should be most concerned about?

5. How have churches served people who live in this area? How might local churches be of service in the future?

6. What impressions, if any, do you have of our church?

Community Resident Interviews

Purpose

Interviewing residents allows you to gain a better understanding of the community and find out more about residents' concerns. It also allows you to demonstrate interest in them on behalf of the church. You may have an opportunity to learn more about them, describe the ministries of your church, or help them deal with a spiritual issue. Interviewers need to be sensitive to the Spirit's leadership after the initial questions have been asked. This kind of interview is different from a thorough information-gathering canvas, a comprehensive publicity effort, or a door-to-door out-reach activity (all of these approaches may be appropriate at other times).

Methods

1. Determine your target area(s).

2. The interviews should be conducted in pairs if possible. Gather the entire interview team and review the objectives and methods. Then divide the area among the teams.

3. It is better to talk with a representative sample of the residents over a broad area than to try to contact everyone in a small area. For example, you might select representative streets in several different neighborhoods and agree on a designated pattern for each street (like every second, third, or fourth house).

4. Good interviews with twenty to thirty community residents should provide a reasonable range of information. The more interviews, the more accurate and more generalizable the information.

Interview Process

1. Begin the interview by identifying yourself and your church.

2. Clarify your purpose. ("We're very interested in the people who live in this neighborhood. If you have a few minutes, I'd like to ask what you think the people of this community are most concerned about.")

3. If the person agrees, allow the interviewee to speak freely while you take notes. Don't interrupt except to clarify a response.

4. Ask if the person regularly attends a local congregation.

5. Offer to respond to questions. ("Is there anything you'd like to ask me?") Respond graciously and concisely.

6. You may want to ask whether and how you might pray specifically for this person in the days ahead. (Take notes. You may want to follow up on the request in a couple of weeks.)

7. Let the person know how to contact you if he or she wishes to add comments or prayer requests. (You can do this by leaving a church calling card.)

8. Thank the person for his or her time.

Rationale

There are several reasons for using this style of interview:

- Our understanding of congregations, as shown in the Congregational Bodylife Model (Resource D), assumes that the issues affecting the lives of community residents will have an impact on the church. Even if the church is not prepared to address an issue, it should be aware of these concerns.

- The church may be able to customize or develop ministries in response to expressed concerns.

- Some residents may be angry or at least skeptical about the motives of anyone from a church. They may perceive that churches are only interested in getting something (attendance, time, money) from them. Asking interviewees to express their concerns will often disarm some negative feelings. Interviewees are generally receptive to this approach.

- The very act of identifying yourself with the congregation and of asking about the interviewee's concerns makes a positive impression. Those seeds of appreciation may develop long after the initial meeting.

Resource D

Congregational Bodylife Model

Congregations are complex social systems. It is helpful, if overly simplified, to parallel them to the human body—holistic entities that contain many interactive parts and subsystems. Just as physicians-in-training first learn human anatomy and physiology, church leaders do well to master a broad understanding of how congregations function.

The Congregational Bodylife Model (Figure D.1) diagrams churches by identifying seven major subsystems and key parts within them. The *mission* and *vision* subsystem describes congregational purpose, the ultimate reason being to participate in God's mission in the world that they are called and empowered to join. Church vision is the portion of that missional journey that churches believe God wants them to achieve in a specific context during the next three to five years. The *boundary* subsystem includes two parts: physical boundaries, where churches gather for their activities, and group boundaries, characteristics of the members and shared identity. Every congregation exists in a unique *context* made up of a local community, the broader culture, and religious networks.

Congregational *heritage* includes everything related to the congregation's past: members' journey with God and one another, their history as an organization, and how they've interacted with their context over the years. The *leadership* subsystem deals with how they are currently relating

FIGURE D.1   Congregational Bodylife Model

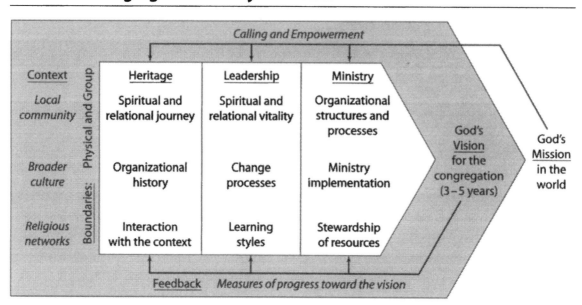

to God and one another, making changes, and learning. *Ministry* involves the ways churches actually implement ministries, use various support structures and processes, and steward resources. *Feedback* describes their progress toward their vision.

Every part and subsystem interacts constantly with every other part and subsystem. However, congregations are more than the mere sum of their parts. They are unique, living bodies that must ultimately be understood and led as holistic systems.

It is also helpful for church leaders to describe what they believe to be the characteristics of an ideal or healthy congregation. An example is offered in Figure D.2; a more thorough treatment of congregational systems can be found in the book.

EXHIBIT D.1   Bodylife Traits of a Healthy Congregation

Mission and Vision

Knows and affirms its biblical mission

Understands clearly God's vision for the congregation

Shares a common interpretation of God's vision

Feels an urgency to respond to God's vision

Focuses on the future

Boundaries

Physical

Meets at an accessible location

Group

Affirms an identity that is distinct from other congregations

Resists undesirable influences from its environment

Works enthusiastically to reach new people

Expresses clear expectations of members and participants

Assimilates new members well

Tries to reduce "dropouts"

Context

Responds properly to changes in its context

Local community

Knows the characteristics and needs of the persons with whom it is called to minister

Recognizes the social structures and dynamics in its community

Broader culture

Understands the implications of cultural changes for ministry

Religious networks

Cooperates actively with other churches and Christian groups

Heritage

Spiritual and relational journey

Celebrates the memories of God's faithfulness and blessings

Has reconciled with God for any past unfaithfulness

Has healed from past conflict among the membership

Organizational history

Affirms specific strengths that the congregation has developed in recent years

Draws from its history in positive ways that enhance learning and high morale

Interaction with the context

Has a good reputation with its community

Leadership

Spiritual and relational vitality

Encounters God in life-changing ways

Displays a spirit of humility and service

Cultivates a strong sense of unity and belonging

Models Christian community that contrasts with the culture

Manages conflict well

Change processes

Demonstrates readiness to make personal changes in light of God's vision

Is guided by a group of trusted leaders

Agrees on how it will achieve God's vision for the next few years

Makes continuous changes in the church that are necessary

Aligns short-term plans and activities with long-term goals

Learning styles

Habitually learns helpful new ways of thinking and acting

Ministry

Facilitates many ways for peoples' lives to be changed by God

Improves the quality of life for persons in its community

Ministry implementation

Develops faithful disciples of Christ who develop other faithful disciples

Experiences inspirational worship together

Has high-quality ministries and programs

Offers effective ministry with persons who aren't members

Organizational structures and processes

Defines clearly the roles and responsibilities of leaders and groups

Distributes authority in satisfactory ways

Communicates well with one another

Makes decisions effectively

Provides many forms of small groups and organizations in which people participate

Stewardship of resources

Inspires members to be good stewards of their time, money, and abilities

Involves members in service for which they are gifted, skilled, and called

Has adequate places for meetings and activities

Feedback

Gathers and uses information on a regular basis about progress toward God's vision

Provides leaders with ongoing feedback that affects their actions

Resource E

Congregational Self-Assessment

Indicate your response to each of the statements below according to how you perceive your congregation at this time, not how you wish it to be. Please circle a number from 1 to 7 for each statement.

	Strongly Disagree						Strongly Agree
MINISTRY							
1. Our church facilitates many ways for people's lives to be changed by God.	1	2	3	4	5	6	7
2. The church has improved the quality of life for people in our community.	1	2	3	4	5	6	7
3. Our congregation develops faithful disciples of Christ who develop other faithful disciples.	1	2	3	4	5	6	7
4. Our worship services are inspirational.	1	2	3	4	5	6	7
5. The church has high-quality ministries and programs.	1	2	3	4	5	6	7
6. The congregation offers effective ministry with people who aren't members.	1	2	3	4	5	6	7
7. We clearly define the responsibilities of church leaders.	1	2	3	4	5	6	7

	Strongly Disagree					Strongly Agree	
8. Authority in our church is appropriately distributed.	1	2	3	4	5	6	7
9. Communication in the church is effective.	1	2	3	4	5	6	7
10. Our congregation makes decisions effectively.	1	2	3	4	5	6	7
11. The church provides many forms of small groups and organizations in which people participate.	1	2	3	4	5	6	7
12. Church members are good stewards of their resources.	1	2	3	4	5	6	7
13. Members of the church serve as leaders in areas for which they are gifted.	1	2	3	4	5	6	7
14. The church's facilities are adequate for its activities.	1	2	3	4	5	6	7

BOUNDARIES

15. Our church's location can be reached easily.	1	2	3	4	5	6	7
16. Our church understands how its personality is different from other congregations.	1	2	3	4	5	6	7
17. We are usually able to keep undesirable practices in our culture from influencing our church's way of doing things.	1	2	3	4	5	6	7
18. We work enthusiastically to reach people.	1	2	3	4	5	6	7
19. Our church clearly describes what it expects of members and participants.	1	2	3	4	5	6	7
20. New members become actively involved in the life of the congregation.	1	2	3	4	5	6	7
21. We try to keep members from dropping out.	1	2	3	4	5	6	7

LEADERSHIP

22. Our leaders regularly encounter God in life-changing ways.	1	2	3	4	5	6	7
23. Our leaders display a spirit of humility and service.	1	2	3	4	5	6	7
24. We cultivate a strong sense of unity in our church.	1	2	3	4	5	6	7
25. We demonstrate Christian community in ways that contrast with the world around us.	1	2	3	4	5	6	7

	Strongly Disagree					Strongly Agree	
26. Our congregation deals with conflict effectively.	1	2	3	4	5	6	7
27. Our leaders demonstrate readiness to make personal changes in their lives in light of God's vision.	1	2	3	4	5	6	7
28. Our church is guided by a group of trusted leaders.	1	2	3	4	5	6	7
29. The members agree on how we are going to achieve God's vision for our church during the next few years.	1	2	3	4	5	6	7
30. The church continually changes what it needs to change to be faithful and effective.	1	2	3	4	5	6	7
31. Our short-term plans are aligned with long-term goals.	1	2	3	4	5	6	7
32. We habitually learn helpful new ways of thinking and acting.	1	2	3	4	5	6	7

CONTEXT

33. Our congregation responds appropriately to changes in its community.	1	2	3	4	5	6	7
34. Our church is aware of the needs of people we are called to reach.	1	2	3	4	5	6	7
35. The congregation understands the social changes in its community.	1	2	3	4	5	6	7
36. Our ministries take into account the cultural changes affecting people's lives today.	1	2	3	4	5	6	7
37. Our congregation cooperates with other Christian groups.	1	2	3	4	5	6	7

MISSION AND VISION

38. Our church knows and affirms its biblical mission.	1	2	3	4	5	6	7
39. Our church clearly understands how God wants our congregation to be different three years from now.	1	2	3	4	5	6	7
40. Most of the members share the same interpretation of God's vision for our church.	1	2	3	4	5	6	7

	Strongly Disagree						Strongly Agree
41. Our congregation displays a strong sense of urgency about achieving God's vision for it during the next few years.	1	2	3	4	5	6	7
42. Most members believe that the best days of our church are in the future.	1	2	3	4	5	6	7

HERITAGE

43. We celebrate the ways that God has blessed our church in the past.	1	2	3	4	5	6	7
44. Our church has asked God to forgive it for specific acts of unfaithfulness in the past.	1	2	3	4	5	6	7
45. Our congregation has healed from past conflict among the members.	1	2	3	4	5	6	7
46. We affirm specific strengths that the congregation has displayed in the past.	1	2	3	4	5	6	7
47. What we have learned from our history as a congregation has helped us become more effective.	1	2	3	4	5	6	7
48. We have a good reputation with our community because of our interaction with it.	1	2	3	4	5	6	7

FEEDBACK

49. The church regularly gathers information about our progress toward God's vision for it.	1	2	3	4	5	6	7
50. The congregation gives leaders on-going feedback that affects their actions.	1	2	3	4	5	6	7

BACKGROUND INFORMATION ABOUT YOURSELF

51. What is the name of the church for which you are filling out this survey?

_____

52. Gender?   ☐ Male   ☐ Female

53. Age?   ☐ 14–17   ☐ 18–24   ☐ 25–34   ☐ 35–44   ☐ 45–54   ☐ 55–64
            ☐ 65–74   ☐ 75+

54. Ethnicity?   ☐ Anglo   ☐ Hispanic   ☐ African American   ☐ Asian
            ☐ Other _____

55. Marital status?   ☐ Single, never married   ☐ Married   ☐ Separated or divorced
            ☐ Widowed

	Strongly Disagree	Strongly Agree

56. If you have children at home, how many are in the following age groups?

___ Less than 4 years   ___ 5–12 years   ___ 13–18 years   ___ no children at home

57. What is your highest level of formal education?

☐ Less than high school   ☐ Some college
☐ Some high school   ☐ College degree
☐ High school graduate   ☐ Graduate or professional degree
☐ Trade or vocational school   ☐ Postgraduate work

58. Are you (check the one that best applies)?

☐ Retired   ☐ Employed part time
☐ Full-time homemaker   ☐ Employed full time
☐ Student   ☐ Unemployed at this time

59. What is your affiliation with this congregation?

☐ First-time or occasional visitor   ☐ Member, 3–5 years
☐ Regular participant, not a member   ☐ Member, 6–10 years
☐ Member, less than one year   ☐ Member, 11–20 years
☐ Member, 1–2 years   ☐ Member for more than 20 years

60. Before attending this congregation, which option below best describes your church participation?

☐ Another church of this denomination   ☐ Visited various churches
☐ A church of a different denomination   ☐ Not active in church for quite some time
☐ A nondenominational church   ☐ Never a member of a church before this one

61. On the average, about how many times did you attend church during the past year?

☐ None   ☐ About once a month
☐ About once or twice a year   ☐ About two or three times a month
☐ About once or twice every 3 months   ☐ Four times a month or more

62. About how many minutes does it take you to travel from home to church on Sunday morning?

☐ Less than 5   ☐ 6–10   ☐ 11–20   ☐ 21–30   ☐ 31–45   ☐ More than 45

63. Describe any changes in your participation in this congregation during the last few years.

☐ Significantly increased   ☐ Increased   ☐ No change   ☐ Decreased
☐ Significantly decreased

64. In how many church organizations, committees, teams, or groups do you hold membership (not counting congregational membership itself)?

☐ None   ☐ One   ☐ Two   ☐ Three   ☐ Four or more

References

Anderson, V., and Johnson, L. *Systems Thinking Basics: From Concepts to Causal Loops.* Cambridge, Mass.: Pegasus, 1997.

Blackaby, H. T., and King, C. V. *Experiencing God.* Nashville, Tenn.: Broadman and Holman, 1990.

Covey, S. A. *The Seven Habits of Highly Effective People: Powerful Lessons in Personal Change.* New York: Simon & Schuster, 1989.

Katzenbach, J. R., and Smith, D. K. *The Wisdom of Teams: Creating the High-Performance Organization.* Boston: Harvard Business School Press, 1993.

Leas, S. B. *Discover Your Conflict Management Style.* (rev. ed.) Bethesda, Md.: Alban Institute, 1997.

Maxwell, J. C. *The Success Journey: The Process of Living Your Dreams.* Nashville, Tenn.: Nelson, 1997.

Ross, R. "The Five Whys." In P. M. Senge and others, *The Fifth Discipline Fieldbook: Strategies and Tools for Building a Learning Organization.* New York: Doubleday, 1994.

Willard, D. *The Divine Conspiracy: Rediscovering Our Hidden Life in God.* New York: HarperCollins, 1998.

The Authors

Jim Herrington is the executive director of Mission Houston, a interdenominational, multicultural group of churches cooperating to complete the Great Commission beginning in the Greater Houston, Texas, area. He earned a B.S. degree (1977) in psychology at the University of Arkansas, Fayetteville, and an M.A. degree in religious education from Southwestern Baptist Theological Seminar in Fort Worth, Texas. Before joining Mission Houston, he served for ten years as the executive director of Union Baptist Association, an association of approximately five hundred churches in the Houston area.

Herrington specializes in pastoral leadership development and leading congregational change. He has consulted with more than one hundred congregations and denominational entities in the areas of congregational transformation, conflict management, leadership development, and spiritual vitality. He is a regular presenter at the Purpose Driven Church seminar on the topic of change leadership.

Mike Bonem is president of Kingdom Transformation Partners, an organization that provides consulting and training assistance to local congregations and denominational entities. He obtained his M.B.A. degree, with distinction, from Harvard Business School in 1985, after having obtained a B.S. degree in chemical engineering from Rice University in 1981.

Bonem's activities have included business consulting with McKinsey and Company and SRI Consulting, and congregational consulting with Union Baptist Association in Houston, Texas. His consulting emphasizes strategy and change leadership, particularly in established organizations. His work with local churches focuses on facilitation of the change process, congregational assessments, vision discernment, and implementation planning. He advocates the adaptation of leading business principles for application by churches. He has also developed and taught seminars on leading congregational change.

Bonem is an active member of a local church and has served as a deacon and a volunteer leader in various aspects of congregational life, including Bible study, finance, human resources, and planning.

James H. Furr is a senior church consultant with Union Baptist Association (UBA) in Houston, Texas; adjunct professor of sociology at Houston Baptist University; and founder of FaithSystems. He earned his B.A. degree (1977) in telecommunications at Texas Tech University in Lubbock; his M.Div. degree (1980) in biblical studies at Midwestern Baptist Theological Seminary in Kansas City, Missouri; and his Ph.D. degree (1987) in church and community studies at Southern Baptist Theological Seminary in Louisville, Kentucky. Prior to his ten years with UBA, he served with Long Run Baptist Association in Louisville for six years and as pastor and church staff person of congregations in Missouri, Kentucky, and Texas.

Furr's major areas of consulting and training include church and community assessment, congregational transformation processes, pastoral leadership development, church conflict management, Christian social ministries, and church consultant development. He is a member of the Religious Research Association and the evangelical Council on Ecclesiology and a participant in the Gospel and Our Culture Network.

To Contact the Authors

To reach the authors for questions or to inquire about support for congregational transformation initiatives:

Mike Bonem or Jim Herrington
Kingdom Transformation Partners
P.O. Box 2272
Bellaire, TX 77402
kingdom-transformation@worldnet.att.net
Phone: (713) 838-9476

Kingdom Transformation Partners provides consulting and training services for individual congregations, denominations, and other Christian organizations. Consulting projects are typically customized to fit the specific needs of the congregation. Other services include teaching seminars on congregational change, leading retreats, supporting denominational or judicatory transformation initiatives, speaking at conferences, and training pastors and other congregational leaders.

Dr. James H. Furr
FaithSystems
9634 S. Kensington Drive
Houston, TX 77031
Phone: (281) 568-3303
E-mail: Furr@faithsystems.com
Website: www.faithsystems.com

FaithSystems provides training and consulting services for congregations, church leaders and faith-based organizations. Training and presentation topics include change leadership skills, dealing with resistance to change, understanding how your church and community really work, the habits of healthy churches, and living God's vision. Consulting services range from short-term assessments to long-term transformation processes.

About Leadership Network

The mission of Leadership Network is to accelerate the emergence of effective churches by identifying and connecting innovative church leaders; providing them with resources in the form of new ideas, people, and tools; and communicating its learnings to the broader church. Churches and church leaders served by Leadership Network represent a wide variety of primarily Protestant faith traditions that range from mainline to evangelical to independent. They are characterized by innovation, entrepreneurial leadership, and a desire to be on the cutting edge of ministry.

Leadership Network's focus has been on the practice and application of faith at the local congregational level. A sister organization, the Leadership Training Network, uses peer learning and interactive training to accelerate the lay mobilization movement and gift-based team ministry.

Established as a private foundation in 1984 by social entrepreneur Bob Buford, Leadership Network is acknowledged as an influential leader among churches and parachurch ministries, and a major resource to which innovative church leaders turn for networking and information.

If you would like additional information on Leadership Network, please contact us directly:

Leadership Network
2501 Cedar Springs
Suite 200
Dallas, TX 75201
800-765-5323
Fax 214-969-9392
Email: info@leadnet.org Website: www.leadnet.org

Made in the USA
Lexington, KY
20 September 2013